THE
NOTION
OF
DIGNITY

Amid Insufficiency and Self-Evident Truths

Dr. Roy Ellis Gaiter, Sr.

i

The Notion of Dignity:

Amid Insufficiency and Self-Evident Truths

Dr. Roy E. Gaiter, Sr.

ISBN: 978-1-73655001- 4

THE
NOTION
OF
DIGNITY

Amid Insufficiency and Self-Evident Truths

Dr. Roy Ellis Gaiter, Sr.

Contents

PREFACE

My loving mother labored many years doing domestic work in various homes. The first time I was able to see where she labored, I was filled with awe as I viewed prosperity. My eyes were opened to a life that was very different from my own.

As a result, I became keenly aware of the disparities of wealth and income. As I observed the abundance of wealth; I sensed that I was living in a world of less. It was as if I had opened a door to a treasure trove of things I could not have or touch -- only observe. It was clearly a shocking contrast to the side of town and the kind of house my family and I lived in, which was typical of the life experienced by many African Americans.

What were the experiences that led African Americans to have less, to be marginalized, working certain jobs, and living in certain neighborhoods? You will find that reading this book will reveal the answers. The Notion of Dignity will be a discovery of why it "was the way it was". It will reveal that kings, lords, peasants, slaves, churches, popes, presidents, businesspersons, slave owners, and lawmakers had a role in the marginalization of enslaved people and their descendants.

This book is the outgrowth of my doctoral work on the impact of poverty among African Americans. Its design is the reality of past and present experiences. Moreover, it is the unearthing of experiences that whispered it didn't have to be the way it was, nor does it have to be the way it is.

The book begins with the notion of dignity in the 1400s, addressing the erosion of dignity that came through discernable legacies of slavery, discrimination, and poverty toward African ancestry, and concludes with a dignity that has no end.

In the beginning, the Creator of mankind endowed humanity with unblemished dignity. Through a faulty human choice, in time, a moral downfall was experienced (Holy Bible, Genesis 1–3).

Ultimately and progressively, this morphed into flawed relationships, such as economic development at the expense of others, i.e., the ranking, grading, and placing humanity in status classifications, and finally through disinterested benevolence regarding human dignity.

The erosion of dignity bafflingly advanced and continued to elevate through life's difficulties. Though dignity has been tarnished, it is not totally demolished.

There is a critical need to revive and restore the damaged and growing aversion to dignity experienced throughout the debauchery of slavery and problems today. Despite slavery the weakened heartbeat of dignity continued to beat. Garbooshian (2006) directly places dignity "at the center of . . . anti-slavery sentiment."

Ken Burns (2009), the award-winning filmmaker, states why he believes the Civil War was inevitable:

We were destined to fight it the second we founded our country. The man who wrote the sentence of the Declaration of Independence that begins, "We hold these truths to be self-evident, that all men are created equal," owned more than 100 human beings. It is, as the great historian Shelby Foote said, "the crossroads of our being."

Roger B. Taney, Chief Justice of the United States Supreme Court in 1857, confirmed what he thought about the contributors of the Declaration of Independence and their intentions when he said, "it is too clear for dispute, that the enslaved African race were not intended to be included, and formed no part of the people who framed and adopted this declaration . . ."

–Roy E. Gaiter, Sr.

ACKNOWLEDGMENTS

I am extremely appreciative for the guidance of the late Dr. George Russell Seay, Jr. Ph.D., and Dr. Leslie Pollard, Ph.D. for their thoughtful and beneficial comments on the writing of this book. Their time and assistance were rewarding in clarifying my thoughts. I would also like to thank Dr. Louis Jenkins, Ph.D. for his valuable and immeasurable insight. In addition, I want to thank Dr. Vincent White, DMin., Stan Patterson, Ph.D., and Skip Bell, DMin. for paving the way before me on this journey.

I am also appreciative of the support and inspiration I received from the members of the Birmingham Ephesus and Norwood churches for the role they played in the garnering of data for my dissertation.

While living in Birmingham, Alabama I was also inspired by having met Fred Shuttlesworth, a civil rights icon and close associate of Dr. Martin Luther King, Jr. Upon his demise I attended Mr. Shuttlesworth's funeral where in attendance were many local, state and federal dignitaries, and civil rights leaders. Having met Mr. Shuttlesworth and having been in the presence of individuals who were actively involved in seeking the dignity of African Americans further reminded me of why dignity is important.

Finally, I would like to thank my wife, Janice, for her support and detailed expertise and the giving of her time on this journey.

My life goes on in endless song,
Above earth's lamentations . . .
How can I keep from singing?

- Robert Lowry

CHAPTER 1

THE EXPLOITATION
OF AFRICAN ANCESTRY

Wealth, income and power are the usual ingredients toward exploitation. Such was the environment of African slavery in the 15th century amongst the Roman Catholic Church and certain Western European countries. The Roman Catholic Church was the richest, predominate power in the 1400s' and used its influence alongside several rulers to support slavery.

Martin Luther would later shine a different light on the unbridled authority of the Catholic Church in the 16th century through the Reformation. However, African slavery, had no such obvious reformer at that time; therefore, African slavery accelerated to be one of the greatest indignities of humanity.

Stuart Anderson (October 24, 2011) writes, "The Pope gave his blessing to the trade in a bull of 1442; enslaving Africans fell within the limits of a 'just war.' This was extended in an edict of 1452, which gave Portugal the right to enslave captives taken in such a war." (p. 1)

Carl Wise and David Wheat (2009) identify what it was like to live at that time:

> Church leaders argued that slavery served as a natural deterrent and Christianizing influence to "barbarous" behavior among pagans. Using this logic, the Pope issued a mandate to the Portuguese king, Alfonso V, and instructed him: . . . to invade, search out, capture, vanquish, and subdue all Saracens and pagans whatsoever ...[and] to reduce their persons to perpetual slavery, and to apply and appropriate to himself and his successors the kingdoms, dukedoms, counties, principalities, dominions, possessions, and goods, and to convert them to his and their use and profit . . ."

On whose authority should a war be waged? Would a war initiated for the purpose of enslaving captives be a "just war"? What makes the war "just"?

The intellectualization of humanness and an egregious economic avarice fueled Western European thought. Intellectualization is a defense mechanism, a deliberate reasoning that removes or blocks feelings about something or someone. In this case it was the blocking of any reasoning that persons of African ancestry were to be valued their full dignity and humanity.

African people became the notion of Western European's aim at procuring slaves for trade and smuggling them to do work involuntarily without compensation. The intellectualization of humanness conceptually provided justification for economic development, but at the cost of human worth that would be exploited, amid contradictions interfering with both relationships and human dignity.

Hakim Adi (2012) writes, "At first this trafficking only supplemented a trade in human beings that already existed within Europe, in which Europeans had enslaved each other."

The negative consequences of Europe's economic development ventures involving African slaves meant indignity for many years to come. Adi (2012) writes this about the slave trade:

> From the middle of the 15th century, Africa entered into a unique relationship with Europe that led to the devastation and depopulation of Africa, but contributed to the wealth and development of Europe. From then until the end of the 19th century, Europeans began to establish a trade for African captives.

In addition to the notion of using African slaves for Europe's economic development, *Europeans also had the notion to change what seemed to them, a people who were "uncivilized," "uncultured," and to bring the "uncultured" to a "dignified" existence.* In fact, Diedrich, M., Gates, L. H. Jr., & Pedersen, C. (1999) contend that:

> the main trajectory of Western European thought

seemed to aim straight toward "some goal" of human cultural progress, undergirded by the "logic" of unbridled economic development . . . Eurocentric and hierarchical concepts of culture and, based on this Eurocentrism, the civilizing mission of Western European culture, relegated Africa to the subordinate position of the Dark Continent, which represented the fallen image of Europe's past, and the Americas to the Virgin Land, which contained the hope for Europe's future.

During the 1960s the notion of Africans being uncivilized was powerfully persuasive. Tarzan was a popular television program in America at that time. The main character, Tarzan, was a white male who was able to swing on vines and yelp in a wide-ranging sound to call elephants, monkeys and other animals of the jungle to his aid when needed. The television program portrayed Africans as *malevolent, uncivilized* people who Tarzan was in conflict with at times in the jungle. Though the program was fictional, it portrayed Africa and Africans in an inferior, unconstructive way.

Western Eurocentrism believed their culture was better, and they tended to impose their culture on other civilizations. Troolin (n.d.), a professor in early European society writes this:

Early modern European society was a hierarchy. Most people identified closely with their social class. They knew where they stood in terms of social class and they lived accordingly, expecting and accepting inequalities as simply a part of life. At the top of the hierarchy stood the nobility [dignity]. Nobles were titled, privileged, and usually wealthy and they owned much of Europe's land. Most nobles inherited their rank from generations of ancestors who had demonstrated their military prowess throughout the Middle Ages, impressing their monarchs and gaining their lands as a reward.

Figure 1.1 features a simple pyramid of what culture was like for people living in the mid-15th to 17th century in Europe. African slaves were considered not at the top or middle; their place was at the bottom of the pyramid. Those previously at the

EUROPEAN DIGNITY PYRAMID

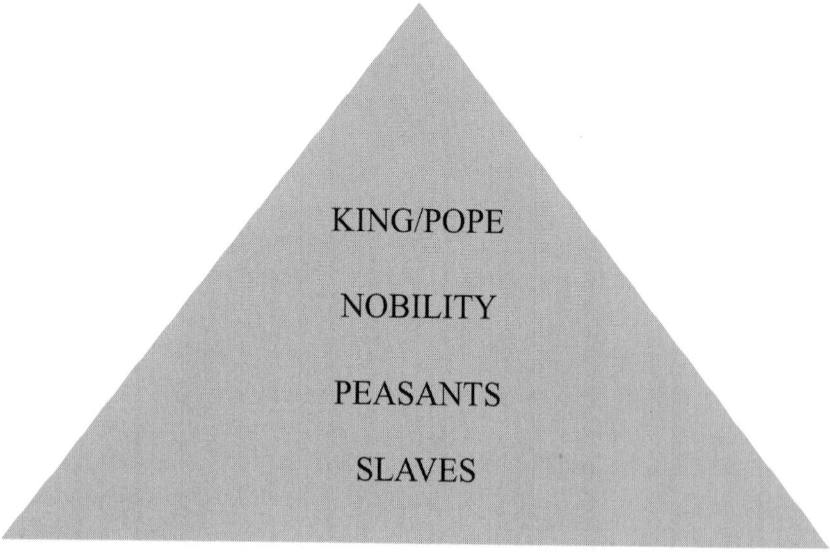

KING/POPE

NOBILITY

PEASANTS

SLAVES

Figure 1.1

bottom were servants, peasants, or indentured slaves.

Upon the arrival of the African slaves, poor peasants became "somewhat" privileged though they remained poor. African slaves were ordered to do work as the peasants and enter the work force at the bottom without recompense.

In this structured hierarchical view, those ranked highest at the top in society were considered those with dignity. Orders of authority from the "elevated ones" were passed downward to be carried out by those under them.

Fagin (n.d.) identifies a protracted relationship of economic poverty and a lack of dignity as human beings were placed into hierarchal racial categories.

> In the 1600s François Bernier was one of the first Europeans to sort human beings into distinct categories. Soon a hierarchy of physically distinct groups (not yet termed races) came to be accepted—with white Europeans, not surprisingly, at the top. Africans were relegated by European observers to the bottom, in part because of (black) Africans' color and allegedly primitive culture, but also because Africans were often known to Europeans as slaves. Economic and political oppression resulted in a low position in the white classification system, or what can be termed racial subordination.

The French lawyer Charles Loyseau (1564–1627) classified

people into different ranks for "social constancy," but these ranks were later eliminated. However, the hierarchal concept remained for many years both in the minds of those who considered themselves elevated and adversely in the experiences of African ancestry. Loyseau (1987) writes the following:

> Because we cannot live together in equality of condition, it is necessary that some command and others obey ... Sovereign lords command all within their state, addressing their commands to the great; the great [address their commands] to the middling, the middling to the small, and the small to the people ... Thus by means of these multiple divisions and subdivisions, the several orders make up a general order, and the several Estates a state well ruled. (p. 14)

This is an example of how European culture was applied to what was deemed an African "cultured problem." Subsequently, African slaves were regarded as "inferior" and were controlled at the bottom and regulated.

Hakim Adi (2012) believes, "The unequal relationship that was gradually created as a consequence of the enslavement of Africans was justified by the ideology of racism—the notion that Africans were naturally inferior to Europeans." Africans were the subordinates, constantly subjected to an illusory European change of progressive dignity.

The terms "cultural progress" and "economic development" used in the context of slavery by Western Europeans were deceptive *sterilized* terms. When "cultural progress" was used in this way, it presented the idea that something was inherently wrong with Africans, and economic development intentionally meant, exploitation and dishonesty.

It was misleading to label the people of Africa as lacking culture and structure. Some of their communities were governed in a more egalitarian manner as councils organized around family and tribal units. Long before the European notion of "human cultural progress," Africans ruled kingdoms. In fact, at one time ancient Egypt was the distinguished civilization in the Mediterranean world.

There were educated African people in Egypt; pharaohs, kings, queens, and mathematicians, and they were skilled in writing, pictorial languages, artistry, and music. They also enjoyed the treasurers of vast economies. There were also other countries in Africa that possessed these achievements.

Joshua J. Mark (2009) writes, "The Great Pyramid at Giza was constructed between 2584 and 2561 BCE for the Egyptian Pharaoh Khufu (known in Greek as 'Cheops') and was the tallest manmade structure in the world for almost 4,000 years." The Great Pyramid is still one of the Wonders of the World.

Africa is a continent with many countries within its borders. Its size in area is often underestimated, and maps of its actual size are disproportionately changed when produced. Africa is actually so vast that many countries would fit into it such as: The United States, Spain, Ireland, Germany, France, Norway, Columbia, Finland, Greece, Italy, Turkey, Poland, China, Ukraine, India and the United Kingdom combined.

Under the European scenario of "human cultural progress," African slaves would naturally question their status as the "lowest" on the European hierarchal social ladder.

A sustained low status is certain to cast doubts about the abilities of Africans. As a result, "unequal relationships" prevented African slaves from performing on "higher levels" to the estimation of others and this false conviction would be passed down through the years. These misgivings affected the thinking of slaves as well.

The ensuing so-called "cultural progress" to the top of the hierarchal ladder was not happening for the African slaves. Instead, it worsened, and they became known as chattel—an item of property.

The slave trade in Europe was well into existence before the first slaves came to the shores of Virginia. European countries amassed numerous slave ships that were used to transport the abducted slaves across the vast ocean.

Several countries participated in the slave trade; however, the following became key transporting competitors: Portugal (Portuguese), Netherlands (Dutch), Britain, Spain, France and Denmark (Danish).

Battles (n.d.) writes for the Low Country Digital History Initiative on the Trans-Atlantic slave trade with this comment:

> The Portuguese dominated the early trans-Atlantic slave trade on the African coast in the sixteenth century . . . After Portugal temporarily united with Spain in 1580, the Spanish broke up the Portuguese slave trade monopoly by offering direct slave trading contracts to other European merchants. Known as the asiento system, the Dutch took advantage of these contracts to compete with the Portuguese and Spanish for direct access to African slave trading, and the British and French eventually followed. By the eighteenth century, when the trans-Atlantic slave trade reached its trafficking peak, the British (followed by the French and Portuguese) had become the largest carriers of enslaved Africans across the Atlantic. The overwhelming majority of enslaved Africans went to plantations in Brazil and the Caribbean, and a smaller percentage went to North America and other parts of South and Central America.

Slaves were kidnapped from various areas of Africa and traded by the Europeans and intermittently with the participation of other Africans. It is estimated that the number of slaves

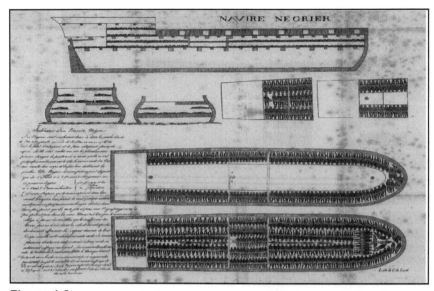

Figure 1.2

The Granger Collection, New York (retrieved from Britannica.com)
This engraving from 1790 shows a diagram of how to pack slaves into a ship.

kidnapped and traded was in the millions.

Countless numbers of slaves did not endure the long voyages. Their health issues were not attended to, therefore many died on the way to their destination. Slave ships were packed with human beings who were chained in the lowermost part of the ship with limited space between them. Was this the declared notion of dignity that Europeans had in mind for the development of its economy?

The depth of inconsideration and disregard for slaves was insurmountable, and the impact on the people of Africa was devastating. The experience of suffering mentally, physically, and emotionally can be seen through these words from

11

the *Transatlantic slave trade slavery and remembrance* (n.d.):

> The transatlantic slave trade can be understood through the experiences of a single enslaved person who endured a series of catastrophic events that, by design, severed him or her from home, family, and nearly all things familiar. Capture in the African interior, transport to the coast, sale to slave traders, passage in a slave ship, and sale and enslavement in the Americas tested the spirit and will of resilient men, women, and children who struggled to find meaning and happiness in a New World dependent upon their labor and coercion. Prior to the full slave market in America most slaves were taken to Brazil and Caribbean Islands such as Barbados, Jamaica, and Haiti. Sugar was a major crop in these areas that made slave trafficking profitable for the countries that employed them.

The Transatlantic slave trade slavery and remembrance (n.d) article continues:

> In time, planters sought to grow other profitable crops, such as tobacco, rice, coffee, cocoa, and cotton, with European indentured laborers as well as African and Indian slave laborers. Nearly 70 percent of all African laborers in the Americas worked on plantations that grew sugar cane and produced sugar, rum, molasses, and other by-products for export to Europe.

Pathetically, these human beings were taken from their families never to see them or their homeland again.

Slaves were stripped of decision-making, and they did not get the chance to choose who their captors or masters would be. They were sold as property, committed to forced labor and often disappeared as if they never existed. Upon their deaths, countless numbers of slaves were not afforded the dignity of grave markers at their burial sites. In the name of economic development and hierarchal dignity, they never received just compensation for developing the economy of others (see Figure 1.3).

The desire to acquire money at any cost was intoxicating and brutal. Slavery of Africans was perhaps the greatest

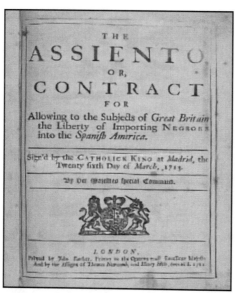

Rockefeller Library Special Collection (retrieved from slaveryandremembrance.org) **The Assiento, or Contract, allowed the subjects of Great Britain to import Negroes into the Spanish America. London, 1713.**

Figure 1.3

evil ever to assail humanity by mankind. There was no pause or stop button that slave traffickers were willing to push.

Dr. Hakim Adi (2012) details the scope of exporting slaves:

> The Spanish took the first African captives to the Americas from Europe as early as 1503, and by 1518 the first captives were shipped directly from Africa to America. The majority of African captives were exported from the coast of West Africa, some 3,000 miles between what is now Senegal and Angola, and mostly from the modern Benin, Nigeria and Cameroon. European nations valued the American slave trade for its potential for economic development and Spanish ships had already touched the American shores. The British however founded the first English colony in 1607.

As an institution the Catholic Church participated in the slave trade as well. Brown (2018) writes about the influence of the church, "The five major countries that dominated slavery and the slave trade in the New World were either Catholic or still retained strong Catholic influences including: Spain, Portugal, France, and England, and the Netherlands."

Williams (2020) details how this happened.

> In the 15th century, the Catholic Church became the first global institution to declare that Black lives did not matter. In a series of papal bulls beginning with Pope Nicholas V's Dum Diversas (1452) and including Pope Alexander VI's Inter

Caetera (1493), the church not only authorized the perpetual enslavement of Africans and the seizure of "non-Christian" lands, but morally sanctioned the development of the trans-Atlantic slave trade. This trade forcibly transported at least 12.5 million enslaved African men, women and children to the Americas and Europe to enrich European and often Catholic coffers.

Williams (2020) is not finished and adds these details:

It also caused the deaths of tens of millions of Africans and Native Americans over nearly four centuries. In the land area that became the United States, the Catholic Church introduced African slavery in the 16th century long before 1619. In fact, at various moments in American history from the colonial era to the U.S. Civil War, the church was the largest corporate slaveholder in Florida, Louisiana, Maryland, Kentucky and Missouri. We must also never forget Roger B. Taney, the nation's first Catholic Supreme Court Justice and a descendant of prominent Catholic slavers from Maryland, infamously declared that Black people "had no rights which the white man was bound to respect," while denying the freedom petitions of Dred and Harriet Scott and their two daughters in 1857.

Williams (2020) continues regarding life and dignity: "The church egregiously violated these teachings through its participation in the trans-Atlantic slave trade and imperial practices of African slavery and segregation in the Americas, Europe and Africa."

In America, according to *A History of Jamestown* (n.d.), the founding of the colony was underwritten by a group of investors.

> The founding of Jamestown, America's first permanent English colony, in Virginia in 1607 – 13 years before the Pilgrims landed at Plymouth in Massachusetts – sparked a series of cultural encounters that helped shape the nation and the world . . . The colony was sponsored by the Virginia Company of London, a group of investors who hoped to profit from the venture. Chartered in 1606 by King James I, the company also supported English national goals of counterbalancing the expansion of other European nations abroad, seeking a northwest passage to the Orient.

Figure 1.4
The Granger Collection, New York (retrieved from pbs.org)
Painted by Robert Lindneux in 1942, *The Trail of Tears*
depicts the suffering of the Cherokee people on the forced march.

The ambitions for economic development that occurred in Europe was later practiced in America. The Native "Indians" in America were adversely impacted by those ambitions as well and their way of life in their native land changed. They were not exported as the Africans were from their homeland, but they were displaced and forced to dwell on reservations. The source, *History: The Trail of Tears Removal Act* (Updated: July 7, 2020) gives this disturbing comment.

> Some officials in the early years of the American republic, such as President George Washington, believed that the best way to solve this "Indian problem" was simply to "civilize" the Native Americans. The goal of this civilization campaign was to make Native Americans as much like white Americans as possible by encouraging them convert to Christianity, learn to speak and read English and adopt European-style economic practices . . ."

The "Indian problem" according to the same source, was that settlers saw Indians as "alien people who occupied land that white settlers wanted".

The history of the relocation of Indians by President Andrew Jackson is detailed in How American Indians Reservations came to be by Elliott (2016) in this way:

> Tens of thousands of Native Americans were relocated to Indian Territory (to an area now part

of Oklahoma) throughout the 1830s. Some tribes left without conflict, but many were ultimately driven by force from their ancestral land. In the North, Shawnees, Hurons, Ottawas, Miamis, Delawares, and others endured the journey west, while in the South, members of the Cherokee, Choctaw, Chickasaw, Creek, and Seminole tribes were among the migrating masses. Most members of the Cherokee Nation were forcibly removed from parts of North Carolina, Tennessee, Georgia, and Alabama on what they called The Trail of Tears. Many became ill and thousands died during the arduous crossing.

What began on the European continent made its way across the Atlantic Ocean. The Native Americans discovered that the notion of dignity did not apply to them either. Instead, it worsened; The Trail of Tears became their devastating "Middle Passage."

When any human is seen as inferior to other human beings and perceived as candidates for economic exploitation, they are priced, labeled for sale; abused and branded—expendable. In essence this changes what human beings are created for.

CHAPTER 2

SLAVERY IN AMERICA

Flagrant efforts were carried out to expand and justify the horrors of slavery, thus continuing the erosion of the dignity of enslaved Africans. Their indignity was propagated and promoted by a degenerate morality and a dishonest *economic policy* assisted by the government. These travesties are the focal points of this section.

In the first chapter the *first notion* was that *Africans would be exploited and used as human instruments for economic development.* In this chapter, that notion is expanded and confirms the truth of what the Bible says, "For the love of money is the root of all evil (1 Timothy 6:10). Enslaving Africans for the love of money was inhumane and evil.

Asserted by some sources, African slaves first disembarked a ship in the early 1600s, facing the further stripping away of their dignity. However, the first African to come to America according to another source was not a slave, at least not in the traditional sense. The date of his coming was 1528, which predates the Dutch ship of 1619, and is reported to be the first ship to bring African slaves.

In the civil liberty source, Head (n.d.) states this:

> A Moroccan slave named Estevanico arrived in
> Florida as part of a group of Spanish explorers
> in 1528; he became both the first known African
> American and the first American Muslim. Es-
> tevanico functioned as a guide and translator, and
> his unique skills gave him a social status that very
> few slaves ever had the opportunity to attain.

The 1619 Project states that about twenty enslaved Africans
were taken from the Congo area and arrived at Point Comfort
Virginia in 1619. This date is before the Pilgrims landing in
New England on the Mayflower in 1620. This is significant
because unlike the Pilgrims, this historical fact was not given
the same credit in the making of America.

In the Smithsonian Magazine, Michael Guasco (2017)
writes the following:

> As early as May 1616, blacks from the West Indies
> were already at work in Bermuda providing expert
> knowledge about the cultivation of tobacco. There
> is also suggestive evidence that scores of Africans
> plundered from the Spanish were aboard a fleet
> under the command of Sir Francis Drake when he
> arrived at Roanoke Island in 1586. In 1526, en-
> slaved Africans were part of a Spanish expedition
> to establish an outpost on the North American
> coast in present-day South Carolina.

In spite of the various dates given as to when Africans came to American soil, what is factual is that most, if not all were taken by force from the soil of the African continent and suffered grim details of the dreadful Middle Passage (the journey from Africa to the Americas).

Diedrich, Gates, and Pedersen (1999) reveal

> the injustice and brutality of tight-packing is unquestionable, the suffering and horror experienced by the slaves is unimaginable. Added to that image was the lack of proper diet, the unhygienic conditions that prevailed aboard the ships, affecting slave and crew alike" (p. 6).

Some suggest the first servants were in the category of "indentured servants" rather than slaves; though another source says it was likely to have been both. The term "indentured servant" means something different than slavery. The difference between "slaves' and "indentured servants" is annunciated in, PBS.org (n.d.) "Africans in America,"

> It's not clear if the Africans are considered slaves or indentured servants. (An indentured servant would be required to work a set amount of time, then granted freedom.) Records of 1623 and 1624 list them as servants, and indeed later records show increasing numbers of free blacks, some of whom were assigned land. On the other hand, records from gatherings do not indicate the marital status of the Africans (Mr., Miss, etc.) and, unlike white

servants, no year is associated with the names – information vital in determining the end of a servant's term of bondage. Most likely some Africans were slaves and some were servants. At any rate, the status of people in bondage was very confusing, even to those who were living at the time.

The full degree of slavery soon followed, thereby eroding dignity. According to Boxill, (as quoted in Meyer and Parent, 1992) slavery, whether sold into it, or forced, is without justification, "Any attempt to mount a case for black slavery would involve so blatant a contradiction that in the words of Locke it would have to be put down as an 'exercise of wit'" (p. 111).

Such justifying of slavery amounts to overlooking one's own need to be free; it is a contradiction, amounting to unreasonable humor. It is humorous to the degree of unthinkable, to make a justifiable case for someone else's slavery; given one's own humanity and overwhelming desire to be free.

To add to this sentiment, passion for freedom was already present when one considers an article by Sylvester (1998).

> Slavery as an issue in America was in constant conflict with the founding Democratic principles of this nation. Slavery therefore became the ultimate test of disunity within the union of states which were already at odds in a democracy es-

pousing freedom for its people. At the center of this conflict were the Africans who were bought, sold, and used as workers on American soil.

Freedom was what early settlers wanted for themselves when they fled British dominion and control. Therefore, it is a "blatant paradox" to support slavery when slaves desired their freedom and dignity, and yet, it was condoned—an example of intellectualization of humanness.

Toni Morrison wrote the award-winning novel Beloved. It was based on the real-life tragedy of a slave woman

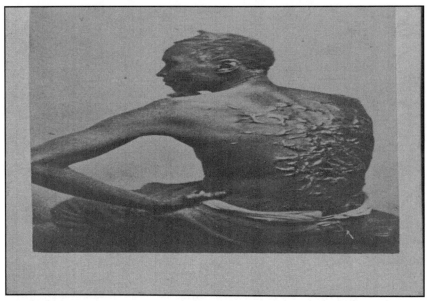

Figure 2.1

charged with murder for the killing of her daughter, or invalidly, she could have been charged for destroying property. Scott (2010) details what transpired:

> In pre-Civil War America, few slave stories were more compelling than Margaret Garner's. She and her family were owned by a Kentucky plantation farmer, but one night they escaped to Ohio with another group of slaves. Their hiding place was discovered, and Margaret's family was surrounded. She swore she would kill her children and herself rather than return to slavery.

What would move a mother to make such choices? There can be no doubt about slavery's heinous atrocities. Slaves did not desire slavery, they despised it, and when you think this event couldn't get any worse, Scott (2010) continues the narrative:

> As her husband was dragged off, Margaret plunged a knife into her daughter. She was preparing to kill her other daughter and herself when she was seized and jailed. Margaret was put on trial. Abolitionists wanted her tried for murder, which would have set a number of precedents, including establishing an enslaved person's rights and responsibility regarding her own children. Instead, Margaret Garner was accused of destruction of property, and sent back into slavery, along with her husband. Her story advanced the rift between the abolitionists and the defenders of slavery, a rift that would soon help lead to the Civil War.

According to Victor Kappeler, professor of the School of Justice studies at Eastern Kentucky University,

> The use of patrols to capture runaway slaves was one of the precursors of formal police forces, especially in the South. This disastrous legacy persisted as an element of the police role even after the passage of the Civil Rights Act of 1964 . . . Questions still arise today about the disproportionately high numbers of people of African descent killed, beaten, and arrested by police in major urban cities of America.

Human dignity is essential to life. So much so that Garbooshian's (2006) dissertation abstract, states, "The central focus of the international Enlightenment is not a move toward secularism but consists instead in the underlying belief in human dignity."

In essence, instead of religion being excluded from schools and society where science and reason was expanding, the idea of human dignity was taking a leading role. Garbooshian insists human dignity was, "at the center of religious thought, views on the place of religion in the state and in society, virtue, self-reliance, and anti-slavery sentiment." The idea of human dignity was prominent, whether one was pro-slavery or anti-slavery, and captured a leading role in debates.

The drafting of the Constitution of the United States reflected the climate of the times as African slaves were looked

Figure 2.2

**William Lloyd Garrison and the Executive Committee of the
Pennsylvania Anti-Slavery Society, 1851.**

upon with disdain. Although political maneuvering by southern slaveholders who wanted to maintain the trafficking of slaves for economic goals existed there were however a few drafters of the Constitution who did not have that mindset. The Anti-Slavery Society worked to persuade white Southerners of the inhumanity of slavery.

According to "Constitutional Topic" (n.d.), "Southern delegates had one thing in mind when it came to slavery: to keep it going to prop up the Southern economy. Indeed, many of the largest slave holders in the United States were at the Convention."

The early Constitution became a pivotal document. It established who had dignity and rights as people and became the center of debate over whether it was a pro-slavery or an anti-slavery document.

Finkelman (2000), an expert on slavery and law, has written many books and scholarly articles. In one article from The U.S. National Archives and Records Administration entitled *Garrison's Constitution: The Covenant with Death and How It Was Made*, conveyed that William Lloyd Garrison, an abolitionist, called the Constitution in its earlier form prior to later Amendments [13th – 15th Amendments], a "covenant with death" (p. 1). Finkelman also says in the same government source that "part of Garrison's opposition to continuing the Union stemmed from a desire to avoid the corruption that came from participating in a government created by the pro-slavery Constitution" (p. 1).

The reason the early Constitution of 1787 was so objectionable and considered a pro-slavery document to Garrison, is that *it would allow slavery and the degrading economic evil offenses to continue, assuring by law, slavery through the Constitution; leaving no end in sight to abolishing it.*

Finkelman (2000) says that Wendell Phillips, a graduate of Harvard converted to the antislavery organization through the efforts of William Lloyd Garrison. Wendell Phillips wrote in 1845 what happened in later years after the Constitution was adopted.

> The slaves trebling in numbers-slaveholders monopolizing the offices and dictating the policy of Government-prostituting the strength and influ-

ence of the Nation to the support of slavery here
and elsewhere-trampling on the rights of the free
States, and making the courts of the country their
tools. (p. 2)

In essence, Phillips says the slave trade increased exponential-
ly to secure economic prominence. Those who owned slaves
also held offices in government. They used their influence to
assure slavery in the nation, despite the concerns of the Free
States (states where slavery was illegal).

During the Convention of 1787 there was considerable
discussion regarding the apparent positioning by Northern and
Southern states, thereby influencing slavery and the Constitution. In the end, the slaveholders received much of what they
wanted but were less conciliatory to the other side.

The following section is an interchange from a transcript of the 1787 Constitution. The Charters of Freedom contains the specific clauses in the 1787 Constitution that impacted slavery. Following each transcript is an interpretation that
comes from Finkelman's article on Garrison's Constitution.
The Charters of Freedom transcript of the Constitution of the
United States in its original form reveals this record:

1. Art. I, sec 2, par. 3. Representatives and direct
Taxes shall be apportioned among the several
states which may be included within this Union
according to their respective Numbers, which

shall be determined by adding to the whole Number of free Persons, including those bound to Service for a term of years, and excluding Indians not taxed, three fifths of all other Persons. (p. 1)

Finkelman (2000) comments on the above portion of the constitution when he says, *"The three-fifths clause provided for counting three-fifths of all slaves for purposes of representation in Congress"* (p. 4). In addition, the states that had the most slaves were the southern states. The contribution of "direct tax" could only be assessed to three-fifths of all slaves for that state (p. 4). *What is noticeable is the fact that slaves were not economically benefited in the increasing of the numbers. They had no representation to vote in Congress and no one would speak up or vote for them to have a better existence.*

What this means is that the Southern slave states benefited by having more representation because of the slave trade; however, the Southern states would only be taxed three-fifths when it came to counting slaves, which was a dishonorable yet privileged benefit for those states that had slaves.

From the Charters of Freedom transcript of the Constitution of the United States, the transcription speaks on the migration and importation of slaves.

2. Art. I, sec 9, par. 1.The Migration or Importation of such Persons as any of the States now existing shall think proper to admit, shall not be

prohibited by the Congress prior to the Year one thousand eight hundred and eight, but a Tax or duty may be imposed on such Importation, not exceeding ten dollars for each Person. (p. 4)

Finkelman (2000) comments on the above constitution,

this clause prohibited Congress from banning the "Migration or Importation of such Persons as any of the States now existing shall think proper to admit" before the year 1808 . . . the clause prevented Congress from ending the African slave trade before 1808 but did not require Congress to ban the trade after the date." (p. 4)

This was significant for it provided the avenue for slavery to continue. Even after the date of 1808 there was nothing in writing that gave Congress the power to discontinue slavery.

Again, the Charters of Freedom transcript of the Constitution of the United States speaks on fugitive slaves.

3. Art IV, sec 2, par. 3. No Person held to Service or Labour in one State, under the Laws thereof, escaping into another, shall, in Consequence of any Law or Regulation therein, be discharged from such Service or Labour, but shall be delivered up on Claim of the Party to whom such Service or Labour may be due. (p. 7)

Finkelman (2000) comments on the above statement from the

30

Constitution when he states, "the fugitive slave clause prohibited the state from emancipating fugitive slaves and required that runaways be returned to their owners "on demand" (p. 4).

Finally, the Charters of Freedom transcript of the Constitution of the United States pronounced,

> 4. Art. V. The Congress, whenever two thirds of both Houses shall deem it necessary, shall propose Amendments to this Constitution, or, on the Application of the Legislatures of two thirds of the several States, shall call a Convention for proposing Amendments, which, in either Case, shall be valid to all Intents and Purposes, as Part of this Constitution, when ratified by the Legislatures of three fourths of the several States, or by Conventions in three fourths thereof, as the one or the other Mode of Ratification may be proposed by the Congress; Provided that no Amendment which may be made prior to the Year One thousand eight hundred and eight shall in any Manner affect the first and fourth Clauses in the Ninth Section of the first Article; and that no State, without its Consent, shall be deprived of its equal Suffrage in the Senate. (p. 7)

Finkelman suggests, "This article prohibited any amendment of the slave importation or capitation clauses before 1808" (Capitation—A Form of Taxation) (p. 4).

Essentially, the laws supported the importation of slaves and changes to the arraignment of dishonest taxation were prohibited before 1808. This demonstrates the desire for power and superiority and to exert it over others. These laws were crafted in the Constitution of the Nation for the purposes of *protecting slavery and maintaining economic position; in turn they would cause death for slaves, prohibit freedom, and erode dignity.*

CHAPTER 3

BETRAYAL OF CIVILITY

Many sunrises and sunsets would come and go without changes in the status and predicament of African slaves. They were considered uncivilized. Uncivilized treatment toward them begs the question, who then are the civilized? There can be no justification of their inhumane treatment. The course of greed and indignity would plunder the nation down a cliff leaving injury and scars to this day. *Hence, the second treacherous notion was the absurdity that Africans and their ancestry were uncivilized, somehow not human.* The reason this notion was so dangerous was that it gave false reasons for the mistreatment of slaves and those of African ancestry.

Elliott (1850) declared how African slaves were treated once they were procured from the African continent whether by force, fraud, or purchased from their land and brought to America:

> The slave markets are very like cattle markets.
> The negroes are there examined like a horse, as to
> soundness of limb and capabilities for toil. They

are exposed to the competitions of purchasers, sold to the highest bidder, and turned over to oppressive labor, under the excitement of the whip. (p. 44)

There was much discussion during the era of slavery over whether African slaves were human or beast. While this debate went on, they were treated as the latter (see Figure 3.1).

Steuter and Willis (2008) observe: "Collars, chains, prods, whips, and branding irons were employed to domesticate and control animals just as similar tactics were used on slaves to ensure they remained docile, subservient and unable to escape" (p. 42).

In addition, Harrold (2005) indicates how Henry Highland Garnett a great orator and black political abolitionist who

Figure 3.1

Retrieved from Revealinghistory.org.uk
Slave shackle, about 1780–1804.

34

lived from 1815–1882 felt about slave masters with these words; "Masters, according to Garnett, sought to make black men 'as much like brutes as possible' by undermining their natural 'love of Liberty,'" their intellects, and their faith" (p. 31). This statement suggests the fulfillment of these words would basically sentence the slave to live without the virtues of humanity. Consequently, leaving African slaves dejected and targeted.

To pro-slavery thinkers, the humanity of Africans was nonexistent, and subjugation was considered moral, as seen in this article by Ross (1990):

> The proslavery rhetorician who grounded his argument in the denial of the humanness of the slave, in the reduction of the slave to a chattel, was insisting on his own innocence. Slavery was not, for him, a matter of subjugation and denial of the principal of freedom. Slavery was instead a natural, even moral, disposition of another species of creature. In this vision, slavery no more tainted the white person than the penning and use of his cattle. (p. 4)

Faced with the erroneous opinions from misguided individuals, African ancestry was considered in some farcical way to be sub-human. To make a step in the right direction prejudiced, misguided individuals should have seen those of African ancestry as their equals, but this was more than they were willing to accept.

Alex Haley's well-known book, *Roots*, was created as a chronicle of his African ancestry. It was later made into a movie revealing slavery in America. For the first time thousands watched the horrible details of slavery previously unknown to many African Americans.

Perhaps the most poignant scene in the saga of *Roots* was when the slave master wanted to break the will of the new slave, Kunta Kinte, by getting him to understand that he would be receiving a "new" name—Toby. Kunta Kinte believed, however, his parents gave him his name at birth. He also believed the Creator God sanctioned it.

In a mini consecration service Kunta Kinte was held up toward the sky on the eighth night after his birth with these words according to Haley (1976), "fend killing dorong leh warrata ka it eh tee (Behold the only thing greater than yourself)" (p. 3). Baby Kunta was linked with God. How could he now deny who he was?

Consequently, Kunta Kinte rebelled because Toby was not the name given him at birth. Toby had no meaning for him. The whip, however, designed to forcibly punish and instruct by means of pain, was applied repeatedly to impose the acceptance of the new name given him in slavery—Toby.

After a bitter resistance, Kunta Kinte finally acknowledged the name forced upon him by the whip. The new African slave was just one of many stripped of their freedom and sense of dignity. With unbearable pain he exhaustedly said, *"My name is Toby."*

After the punisher ceased the beating, the atmosphere remained chaotic and tense as though someone had just been murdered. Then one of the slaves who had been a mentor on the plantation came to console Kunta Kinta. Sympathetic to the horror he had just witnessed he uttered these words, "You know who you be, Kunta; that's who you always be. *Kunta Kinte"* (video source taken from the movie *Roots* on YouTube).

Kunta Kinte's mentor was right theologically, for spiritually when there is an understanding and acceptance of who God is, then one understands better who he/she is. Kunta Kinte knew his name had meaning. He refused to have a name change because he was safeguarding his dignity—protecting his identity. Without family, friends, and familiar surroundings it was all he had left; the dignity of who he was through his name.

The words Kuni, Kunindi, and Kuninta could very well be words from which "Kunta" is a derivative. They are variations of the same meaning to awaken, be awake, or to be aware (Mandinka-English Dictionary, 1995).

While *Roots* was based on real life, all written accounts of the book Roots, the movie, or the name Kunta, cannot be confirmed with certainty. The scene of the name-change, however, captures the essence of African slaves and later African American citizens treated heartlessly denying them civility.

Millions of African Americans have been forced to change the awareness of who they are, or should be in God, to a relegated system of post-slavery, discrimination, incarceration and poverty. Their existence mimics Kunta Kinte being forced to become Toby, being stripped of his dignity, and being looked upon and locked up as mere property.

Generations after slavery, African Americans were prevented from voting, and when they could lawfully vote they were suppressed from doing so. They were demanded to go to the rear of the bus to be seated. They had to drink from segregated water fountains. They were educated in inadequate schools and told to live in their "own" neighborhoods, separated from whites. Unjust laws made it appear that African Americans were lawbreakers, and it continues to be a problem today.

Slaves who were taught to read or learned on their own became a national security issue. According to Maddox (2009), "Slave codes prohibited all Whites from teaching Blacks how to read and write. Prudence Crandall, a White Quaker teacher, felt the sting for attempting to educate Black girls. For her efforts, her school was burned in Canterbury, CT" (p. 31).

Frederick Douglas (1852) gave details of the unconscionable disregard of slaves and how they were treated. Speaking from the argumentation of irony, Douglas suggests:

Frederick Douglas

> The manhood of the slave is conceded. It is admitted in the fact that Southern stature books are covered with enactments, forbidding, under severe fines and penalties, the teaching of a slave to read or write. When you can point to any such laws in reference to the beast of the field, then I may consent to argue the manhood of the slave. When the dogs in your streets, when the fowls of the air, when the cattle on your hills, when the fish of the sea, and the reptiles that crawl, shall be unable to distinguish the slave from a brute, then I will argue with you that the slave is a man!

Foner (1975) expresses another setback for African slaves in his biography of Daniel Payne (1811–1893) who became the first African American college president in the nation at Wilberforce University.

Foner writes this with reference to Payne:

> In 1826 he joined the Methodist Episcopal Church and three years later opened a school for Negro children, which he conducted until the South

Carolina legislature passed a law, on December 17, 1834, imposing a fine and whipping on free persons of color who kept schools to teach slaves or free Negroes to read or write." (p. 89)

Considering African slaves, as property was a sentiment felt by some who professed to be Christians. This was an attempt unjustifiably so, to "morally" support slavery in the minds of Bible believers, therefore, spiritually sanitizing the erosion of dignity.

When the reading of the Bible was accepted, it became an anchor, a pivotal book for learning. Bost (as cited in Raboteau, 2004) reflects on slaves reading the Bible when he says, "All the readin' they ever hear was when they were carried through the big Bible" (p. 239).

Although enslaved Africans were treated harshly, seasons of worship and ceremonies brought restored glimpses of dignity. Raboteau (2004) says slaves maintained, "in these seasons of celebration that their lives were special, their lives had dignity, their lives had meaning beyond the definitions set by slavery.... And here, too some slaves found the place to exercise their talents for leadership" (p. 231).

These seasons of celebrations were designed to inspire optimism and compassionate concern for those who were considered "the least of these" in society. These celebrations paved the way for hope and worth on a foundation that they were created in the image of God, with the highest dignity, as sons and daughters of God despite past, present, and future injustices.

On the other hand, slavery sympathizers according to Roberts (1974), confirms the Christian environment during slavery was "a clear attempt to theologize the black man into inferiority and theologize the white man into superiority" (pp. 77, 78). Furthermore, Roberts suggests that "slaves, obey your masters" in Colossians 3:22 became a favorite text for slavery preachers and theologians (p. 76).

Boles (1988) affirms with the following:

> Biblical justifications of slavery were increasingly popular as the mainstay of the South's proslavery argument. As masters accepted this defense of their peculiar instruction, they confronted its logical corollary: divinely sanctioned masters have religious obligations to their servants (p. 106).

Gesisler (1971) indicates, "At first glance, the Scriptures may seem to condone forced slavery.... However, it should be noticed that the Bible does not *command* slavery; at best it only permitted slavery" (p. 185).

Longenecker (1992) insists that New Testament Scripture householders "were instructed to treat their slaves with consideration (1 Cor. 7:21–22; Col. 3:22–23). Following Paul's tradition, the early Fathers asserted that the slave and

41

his or her master were equal before God" (p. 386).

Carson (1960) writes on Col. 3:22–24:

> The overriding consideration is the Lordship of
> Christ, which transforms the quality of the ser-
> vice rendered ... It is also noteworthy that in con-
> trast to prevailing practice Paul treats the slaves
> as persons, not as things (p. 93).

Felder (1991) gives an accurate and appropriate summation
when it comes to the Bible and African slavery in America
when he says, "The Bible contains no narratives in which the
original intent was to negate the full humanity of black people
or view blacks in an unfavorable way. Such negative attitudes
about black people are entirely postbiblical" (p. 127).

Many breakthroughs contributed to the final freedom of
slaves when one notable personality emerged; Abraham Lincoln was elected president in November 1860, and challenged
the institution of slavery. When he became president in January
1861, he included this warning to the South in his Inaugural
Address, found on the website, White House Presidents (n.d.):

> In your hands, my dissatisfied fellow country-
> men, and not in mine, is the momentous issue of
> civil war. The government will not assail you . . .
> You have no oath registered in Heaven to destroy
> the government, while I shall have the most sol-
> emn one to preserve, protect and defend it.

Although many people questioned the morality of slavery, the evilness of its existence was so ingrained it would take a Civil War to bring it, to some extent, to an "end." The resolve to maintain the position of slaves as property among slavery sympathizers would produce thousands of deaths among those of the Union States in the North as well as those of Confederate States in the South.

Many presidents before Lincoln enslaved hundreds of human beings. Evan Andrews (2019) article title, "How many U. S. presidents enslaved people" details:

> The "peculiar institution" loomed large over the first few decades of American presidential history. Not only did enslaved laborers help build the White House all of the earliest presidents (except for John Adams and his son John Quincy Adams) owned enslaved people. George Washington kept some 300 bondsmen at his Mount Vernon plantation.

The next president, Thomas Jefferson is well known for fathering several children with his mistress slave Sally Hemings. Evan Andrews (2019) continues,

> Thomas Jefferson—despite once calling slavery an "assemblage of horrors"—owned at least 175 enslaved workers at one time. James Madison, James Monroe and Andrew Jackson each kept several dozen enslaved workers, and Martin Van Buren owned one during his early career. William Henry Harri-

son owned several inherited enslaved people before becoming president in 1841, while John Tyler and James K. Polk were both enslavers during their stints in office. Zachary Taylor, who served from 1849–1850, was the last chief executive to keep enslaved people while living in the White House. He owned some 150 enslaved workers on plantations in Kentucky, Mississippi and Louisiana. Perhaps surprisingly, the last two presidents to own enslaved workers were both men closely associated with Abraham Lincoln, who led the nation during a civil war caused in large part by the divisions sowed by slavery, and later signed the Emancipation Proclamation and championed passage of the 13th Amendment ending slavery. Andrew Johnson, who served as Lincoln's vice president before becoming president in 1865, had owned at least half a dozen enslaved people in his native Tennessee and even lobbied for Lincoln to exclude the state from the Emancipation Proclamation. The last president to personally own enslaved people was Ulysses S. Grant.

Lincoln is again quoted from the source White House Presidents (n.d.) in a dedication address given at Gettysburg cemetery where the two opposing armies of the North and South fought and died as cited:

> That we here highly resolve that these dead shall not have died in vain--that this nation, under God, shall have a new birth of freedom--and that government of the people, by the people, for the people, shall not perish from the earth.

44

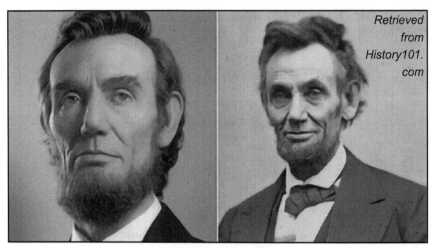

Abraham Lincoln

Lincoln saw the nation deteriorating even before he was president. In a speech from June 1858, in the Illinois statehouse, Lincoln spoke to 1,000 representatives who had chosen him to be their candidate for the U.S. Senate (Abraham Lincoln, n.d.):

> Mr. President and Gentlemen of the Convention. If we could first know where we are, and whither we are tending, we could then better judge what to do, and how to do it. We are now far into the fifth year, since a policy was initiated, with the avowed object, and confident promise, of putting an end to slavery agitation. Under the operation of that policy, that agitation has not only, not ceased, but has constantly augmented. In my opinion, it will not cease, until a crisis shall have been reached, and passed. "A house divided against itself cannot stand." I believe this government cannot endure, permanently half slave and half free.

It should not be assumed that freeing the slaves was the total motivation for the Civil War when Lincoln became president. He wanted to keep the Union together. However, the dignity of slaves was also an undeniable issue that needed to be resolved.

As stated in the preface of this book, Burns (2009), a historical filmmaker, was asked about his fascination with the Civil War. He responded:

> We were destined to fight it the second we founded our country. The man who wrote the sentence of the Declaration that begins, "We hold these truths to be self-evident, that all men are created equal," owned more than 100 human beings. It is, as the great historian Shelby Foote said, "the crossroads of our being." (p. 8)

The signal to end slavery and slow the progression and erosion of dignity would come with the Emancipation Proclamation on January 1, 1863. This meant slaves detained in the slave states of the confederacy were freed to fight for the union.

Slavery in America was demeaning and demoralizing for those who endured it. The Northern states of the country wanted to maintain its "rights and authority" to liberate itself from slavery, while the Southern states wanted to secede from the nation to continue slavery.

It would be impossible for a nation to continue in this

manner when human beings were so marginalized. Therefore, we were doomed to fight the Civil War. President Abraham Lincoln opposed dividing the country and he opposed the mistreatment of slaves. Consequently, the nation was living a hypocritical existence, and a betrayal of civility to its own declaration. Principally there can be no justification for slavery given the reality that all people were created with dignity.

By April 9, 1865, the Civil War had come to an end, thus sending a signal to the sacredness of the lives of slaves, and for the nation to hold its truths sacred, "that all men are created equal."

CHAPTER 4

INJUSTICE AND DISCRIMINATION

With the end of the Civil War, the erosion of dignity continued to plague African Americans in old and new ways. Cozzens (1998) writes, "Although blacks after the Civil War enjoyed freedoms and privileges that their slave ancestors could only dream of, they faced increasing discrimination towards the end of the 19th and the beginning of the 20th century."

The *third notion* of dignity was *that Western Europeans believed they needed to remedy what they judged as "uncivilized" Africans*. This flawed notion was never dispensed with in America. Enslavers and sympathizers of slavery somehow thought they were being *missionary minded* to bring Africans and their ancestry to a place of elevation—to dignity. To show how flawed this notion became, *there were those who thought they did slaves, and now freed African Americans, a favor by enslaving them*. The deceitfulness in this idea was seeing themselves as superiors; therefore, indifference toward others was how they governed. Instead of elevation, segregationists wanted to *keep the now newly freed slaves in their place.*

Discrimination and segregation became acceptable means of accommodating the freed slaves. But dignity and equality remained a crisis for the former slaves. These difficulties of dignity are the focus of this chapter in the African American experience.

The segregated social existence of the "freed" slaves ironically became suppression, and it made their economic development difficult. Laws were enacted called "Black Codes" that prohibited the social dignity of Blacks having equitable existence in society.

Again, Cozzens (1998) shares this account,

> Despite these major improvements, life for Southern blacks was far from perfect. "Black Codes," designed to limit the opportunities of blacks, were passed in the South during Reconstruction. The Black Codes placed taxes on free blacks who tried to pursue nonagricultural professions, restricted the abilities of blacks to rent land or own guns, and even allowed the children of "unfit" parents to be apprenticed to the old slave masters. In effect, this was a continuation of slavery.

Immediately after slavery Black Code Laws were enacted in the North and South to provide social separateness among

"Blacks and Whites," which was antithetical to dignity, restricting opportunities, abilities, and movement. It was difficult for former slave masters and slavery sympathizers to grapple with the idea of former slaves having dignity. Those of African ancestry considered Black Codes as nothing but a continuation of marginalization. The "alleged ending of slavery" instead became an ongoing extension.

Unjustifiable laws such as Black Codes eventually emerged into what is better known as Jim Crow Laws. *These laws were intentionally melded into state and local laws, especially in the South, to give the sense that it was acceptable to treat people of color as second-class citizens; after all it was part of the law.*
The origins of Jim Crow Laws according to Katznelson (2005), suggest it "dates to the caricature of a black by that name first used in 1828, in a minstrel show for white audiences" (Notes, p. 183). These laws were designed to keep African Americans from enjoying their new freedom and to continue deliberate inequality and segregation.

The problem with Jim Crow Laws mentioned by Katznelson (2005), is that it's "a law which forbids a group of American citizens to associate with other citizens in the ordinary course of daily living creates inequality by imposing a caste status on the minority group" (p. 7).

Laws such as these could not help the cause for dignity. In the early post-slavery phase African Americans must begin in a substandard social position, again. Assumed promises toward dignity were virtually non-existent.

Katznelson (2005) further states that the 1947 Committee on Civil Rights was summed up this way:

> Only the termination of segregation in schools, housing, public accommodations, and the armed forces, and only an end to lynching (there were six in 1946), police brutality, the denial of suffrage, and discrimination at work, in healthcare, and public services, the writers argued, could make American democracy whole. (p. 7)

Karon (1975) explains "an elaborate racial etiquette of personal relations governing the actions of blacks and whites when they meet each other, such as the code prescribed by the South" (p. 12).

Such an etiquette code according to Karon was designed "to prevent members of the two castes from knowing each other" (p. 18). Once again, some southerners might say to "keep blacks in their place" —segregated and subordinate.

The Jim Crow etiquette is not the same as Jim Crow Laws, they will be looked at later, but the etiquette laws did go hand in hand with the Jim Crow Laws. How African Americans were to conduct themselves according to the etiquette suggested inferiority, therefore indignity.

The following eight examples by Pilgrim (2000) were a part of the Jim Crow etiquette norms:

1. A Black male could not offer his hand (to shake hands) with a White male because it implied being socially equal. Obviously, a Black male could not offer his hand or any other part of his body to a White woman, because he risked being accused of rape.

2. Blacks and Whites were not supposed to eat together. If they did eat together, Whites were to be served first, and some sort of partition was to be placed between them.

3. Under no circumstance was a Black male to offer to light a cigarette of a White female—that gesture implied intimacy.

4. Blacks were not allowed to show public affection toward one another in public, especially kissing, because it offended Whites.

5. Jim Crow etiquette prescribed that Blacks were introduced to Whites, never Whites to Blacks. For example: "Mr. Peters (the White person), this is Charlie (the Black person), that I spoke to you about."

6. Whites did not use courtesy titles of respect when referring to Blacks, for example, Mr., Miss., Sir, or

Ma'am. Instead, Blacks were called by their first names. Blacks had to use courtesy titles when referring to Whites and were not allowed to call them by their first names.

7. If a Black person rode in a car driven by a White person, the Black person sat in the back seat or the back of a truck.

8. White persons had the right-of-way at all intersections.

Though discrimination existed in the northern states, there is no evidence of such an elaborate etiquette eroding the dignity of African Americans of freedoms and rights as it was in the South.

To ensure the keeping of the etiquette, according to the Ferris State University Educational article, "violence must be used to keep Blacks at the bottom of the racial hierarchy" (p. 2).

Jim Crow Laws instead were exclusionary in nature, according to Simkim (n.d.) who says, "This included laws that discriminated against African Americans with concern to attendance in public schools and the use of facilities such as restaurants, theaters, hotels, cinemas and public baths. Trains and buses were also segregated."

A pivotal decision regarding segregation came from the United States Supreme Court. It was the case of *Plessey v. Ferguson*. Ferguson was a judge in the Orleans District who ruled in a lower court against Plessey. Louisiana state law provided the so called "separate but equal" accommodations for its riders. Plessey challenged this law. He thought himself to be (one eighth) Black, but whose complexion (seven-eighths Caucasian) was considered as White; therefore, he took his seat, in the "White only" section.

Martha Sandweiss explains how "In 1880, at the height of the Jim Crow laws and [the] obsession with defining what black people were, the federal government allowed you on your census form to be white, black, mulatto, quadroon or octoroon." Octoroon means one-eighth. In many cases if a person had one black great-grandparent that person would be considered black by these erronious laws.

A Cornell University (n.d.) source details the decision outcome on *Plessey v. Ferguson* case by the Supreme Court on May 18, 1896, which said,

> that no person shall be permitted to occupy seats in coaches other than the ones assigned to them, on account [p. 538] of the race they belong to; and requiring the officer of the passenger train to assign each passenger to the coach or compartment assigned for the race to which he or she belongs; and imposing fines or imprisonment upon passengers insisting on going into a coach or compartment other than the one set aside for the race to which he or she belongs; and conferring upon officers of the train power to refuse to

carry on the train passengers refusing to occupy the coach or compartment assigned to them, and exempting the railway company from liability for such refusal, are not in conflict with the provisions either of the Thirteenth Amendment or of the Fourteenth Amendment to the Constitution of the United States.

The law sanctioned the erosion of dignity from the highest court of the land, distinguishing some humans as superior and others inferior. This was a racist decision sanctioned by the courts, because some were elevated as superior and assigned seating in a particular location deemed appropriate, while others were deemed inferior and assigned seating in a different location. This fostered an exalted opinion of one, leaving the other devalued.

This legalization of separation would continue for decades. Needless to say, African Americans found it difficult to appeal their dignity, equality, and freedoms in the courts of the southern states.

It would not be until 1954, in the U.S. Supreme Court case of *Brown v. Board of Education*, that successfully challenged laws of "separate but equal" changed in a landmark decision. The case weighed whether or not Black children would be allowed to attend a segregated school in Topeka, Kansas, and similar cases in other states were also scheduled to be challenged.

Find Law (n.d.), a professional source for lawyers, gives these details of the case:

> They had been denied admission to schools attended by white children under laws requiring or permitting segregation according to race. This segregation was alleged to deprive the plaintiffs of the equal protection of the laws under the Fourteenth Amendment.

In the Topeka, Kansas case, *Brown v. Board of Education*, Oliver Brown was the father of one of the children. Brown wanted to enroll his young daughter in school. In the article, "Brown vs. Board of Education" (n.d.), an explanation is given on how his name was selected, "Parents filed suit against the Topeka Board of Education on behalf of their twenty children. Oliver Brown, a minister, was the first parent listed in the suit, so the case came to be named after him."

This case had far-reaching implications toward dignity. African Americans across the country experienced restrictions regarding their abilities, freedoms, and problems, based not on being human but the color of their skin. Brown v. Board of Education (n.d.), characterizes the case as such:

> *Brown v. Board of Education* was not simply about children and education. The laws and policies struck down by this court decision were

products of the human tendencies to prejudge, discrimination, and stereotype other people by their ethnic, religious, physical, or cultural characteristics.

The implementation of dignity for African Americans was constantly elusive; however, in 1954 the United States Supreme Court dismantled America's "apartheid system."

Daugherity and Bolton (2008) wrote about the growing frustrations of ordinary rights. They explained how elusive the implementation of dignity became after the landmark decision, and how it set up the early years of the Civil Rights movement.

The era also witnessed growing black frustrations with the efforts to achieve school integration, which helped to fuel the larger movement of the 1960s. In these ways and others, a better understanding of the state and local campaigns to implement Brown v. Board of Education sheds crucial light on the early years of the civil rights movement in the United States. (p. viii)

According to Daugherity and Bolton, the frustrations after the *Brown v. Board of Education* decision contributed to the fact that "implementation would be left to the federal district courts" (p. viii) of which many African Americans had little or no representation in the southern states.

The United States Capitol building

Daugherity and Bolton added, "The Court also offered an ambiguous timetable for action, urging a vague pace for change with the oxymoron, 'with all deliberate speed'" (p. viii).

With large demonstrations and public marches, the Civil Rights period of the 1960s clearly exposed the need for African Americans to be recognized as human beings.

The Civil Rights Act of 1964 endorsed by the United States Congress was designed to do for society what *Brown v. Board of Education* was designed to do in the educational school system, namely, to integrate and abandon restrictions based on race. Before the passage of the bill, the country maintained a segregated society, especially in the South, which meant inferiority existed, liberties were curtailed, and abilities were denied. These denials were problematic to dignity and impacted poverty.

Loevy (1990) explains how difficult the debate and vote for the Civil Rights Act of 1964. It lasted 83 consecutive legislative days.

> The reason the debate was so long was that the bill that later became the Civil Rights Act of 1964 was subjected to a filibuster by a determined group of Southern senators. Senate rules normally provide for unlimited debate, which means that a small group of senators can attempt to kill a bill by simply talking it to death and not letting it come up for a final vote. As a result of this Southern filibuster, the Civil Rights Act of 1964 was before the Senate for 83 consecutive legislative days—from March 9 to June 17, 1964. (p. 1)

The debate was finally ended by "cloture." According to Loevy, cloture is "a motion to close debate by a 2/3 vote of the Senate. . . .[It was the] first important limitation of debate in the history of the United States Senate. . . . Comprehensive civil rights legislation could not have passed without it" (pp. 1, 2).

One of the cities steeped in the civil rights struggle was Birmingham, Alabama. Birmingham was deep seated in discrimination, earning it the unsavory name of "Bombmingham." Loevy (1990) gives a reason for this. "From 1957 to 1963 there had been some 18 racial bombings, leading many civil rights supporters to call the city 'Bombmingham'" (p. 11). Bombs exploded in African American neighborhoods with the targets being the homes of civil rights leaders and their establishments, including churches.

The President of the United States at that time was John F. Kennedy, and Martin Luther King, Jr. was one of the leaders of the Birmingham demonstrations. Both men contributed to tearing down systems that eroded dignity.

Loevy (1990) observes in 1963, a speech given by Kennedy to the nation describing African Americans as not "fully free." Kennedy said to the nation:

> We are confronted primarily with a moral issue. It is as old as the scriptures and is as clear as the American Constitution.... 100 years of delay have passed since President Lincoln freed the slaves, yet their heirs, their grandsons, are not fully free ... and this nation, for all its hopes and all its boasts, will not be fully free until all its citizens are free. We preach freedom around the world ... but we say to the world ... that this is the land of the free except for Negroes? (p. 17)

The struggle for dignity was brought into the homes of the nation on national television and radio stations at a time when public media had great interest in the protest. Loevy (1990) explains what the nation saw: "Television news film of nonviolent black demonstrators being abused, beaten, and arrested while they sat-in at Birmingham lunch counters, were presented nightly in living rooms across the nation" (p. 15).

Bill Hudson/Associated Press (retrieved from npr.org)
A police dog in Birmingham, Ala., attacks a 17-year-old Civil Rights demonstrator on May 3, 1963. This image led the front page of the next day's New York Times.

President Kennedy wanted to do more to help the cause of civil rights; however, in November 1963 he was killed by an assassin's bullet. Five months before his death, Kennedy had invited Black leaders to meet with him.

Eskew (as cited by Shuttlesworth, 1997) said that Kennedy intimated that if it were not for Birmingham "we would not be here today." If being here meant his presidency, then the struggle for dignity by African Americans played a significant role.

African Americans had grown to distrust the government and law enforcement because local and state governments did not allow peaceful protests for freedom. For example, Tiffany Hagler-Geard (2012 Feb. 12) of ABC news writes, marchers "were attacked by state and local police with weapons and tear gas as they reached the Edmund Pettus Bridge in Selma, injuring 17 protesters in what came to be known as 'Bloody Sunday'." One of the protesters beaten severely was John Lewis who later became United States Congressman from the state of Georgia.

African Americans could not attend institutions of higher learning at some of the state colleges in Alabama and other states. The reason for this was simple, the color of their skin mattered. Had they been White, they would have been received with opened arms. Discrimination and racism are blind guides which should not be adhered to.

According to Debbie Elliott (2003, June 11), Alabama's Governor, George C. Wallace, expressed his position on June 11, 1963, as he "stood at the door of Foster Auditorium at the University of Alabama in a symbolic attempt to block two black students, Vivian Malone and James Hood, from enrolling at the school." According to a NPR article (2013 January 10) titled "Segregation Forever," Wallace vowed on January 14, 1963 in an earlier inaugural address, "segregation now, segregation tomorrow, and segregation forever."

Corky Siemaszko (2012 May 3) explains, from "May 2 to May 10, 1963, the nation bore witness as police in Birmingham, Ala., aimed high-powered hoses and . . . dogs on black men, women and even children" under the orders of Bull Connor, who was then the commissioner of public safety.

In addition, an article called "Equal Access to Public Accommodations" (n.d.) from a Virginia historical society states, "Blacks could not use restaurants, bathrooms, water fountains, public parks, beaches, or swimming pools used by whites. They had to use separate entrances to doctor's offices and sit in separate waiting rooms."

Obstacles that prevented them from voting hampered the dignity of African Americans in the South. In "American Government Obstacles to Voting" (n.d.), the difficulties were visibly seen. "Southern states charged a fee before a person could vote, and a few added the unpaid fees from one election to another."

Again, in the Southern states, literacy tests were used to restrict applicants. The usual practice was to require an African American to explain some complex part of the Constitution, while whites were given an easier passage to read and explain.

There were other contingencies cited in the same source such as "an endorsement of a good character from two or more registered voters." They had to give proof that a father or grandfather had voted before and proof of residency for living in the community for a certain length of time. These were all done to prevent African Americans from voting. Unfortunately, voter suppression continues today.

After Kennedy's death, Martin Luther King Jr., would continue to discuss the need for dignity for all people with President Lyndon Johnson. It was Johnson, not Kennedy, who signed the Civil Rights Act that abandoned legalized segregation. Johnson was also instrumental in gaining the passage of the Voter's Right Act. According to the "Civil Rights Division" (n.d.),

> African Americans were substantially disfranchised in many Southern states, the Act employed measures to restore the right to vote that intruded in matters previously reserved to the individual states. Section 4 ended the use of literacy requirements for voting in six Southern states (Alabama, Georgia, Louisiana, Mississippi, South Carolina, and Virginia) and in many counties of North Carolina, where voter registration or turnout in the 1964 presidential election was less than 50 percent of the voting-age population.

More than any other achievement, President Johnson wanted to wage war on poverty. He wanted to create what he termed "The Great Society."

Gardner (n.d.) suggests, "Johnson wanted to create the 'Great Society'—to end poverty, promote equality, improve education, rejuvenate cities, and protect the environment."

Johnson's plan was ambitious, and perhaps would have

brought about a greater transformation on the war on poverty if it had not been for the war, in Vietnam, which cost billions of dollars to sustain.

The Vietnam War was a war that Johnson inherited. Johnson was compelled to make a choice between the War on Poverty and the Vietnam War. It is said that he chose both—and would win neither (*L.B.J. PBS American Experience*).

The lack of resources continues to be a crisis in American society. With slavery over and laws instituted to minimize observable discrimination, poverty was the next hindrance toward dignity. Poverty continues to be the residual effect, and it remains an obstruction to dignity.

CHAPTER 5

POVERTY AND INCARCERATION

As set forth in this book, African Americans battled through slavery and discrimination. This chapter's focus will cover the erosion of dignity among African Americans as it relates to their *poverty and incarceration, highlighting the taste of inequalities and the indifference toward any notion of advancement.* Blacks were considered great workers but later viewed as a criminal race; an idea clearly seen in the judicial system, law enforcement, and political arenas today.

African Americans were enslaved after the Civil War as "criminal slaves". The documentary *Slavery By Another Name* captures the essence of how this was accomplished with the support of the judicial system, law enforcement, and by political means. Whitney Benns (2015 September) asks and adds this information from the Atlantic magazine,

> Didn't the Thirteenth Amendment abolish all forms of slavery and involuntary servitude in this country? Not quite. In the shining promise

of freedom that was the Thirteenth Amendment, a sharp exception was carved out. Section 1 of the Amendment provides: "Neither slavery nor involuntary servitude, except as punishment for crime whereof the party shall have been duly convicted, shall exist within the United States, or any place subject to their jurisdiction." Simply put: Incarcerated persons have no constitutional rights in this arena; they can be forced to work as punishment for their crimes.

Regarding poverty, African Americans retain a higher percentage of poverty than all ethnic groups in America. During the time of the Vietnam War, Dr. Martin Luther King, Jr., as seen on YouTube (n.d.) suggested in a speech on April 30, 1967, "It is estimated that we spend five hundred thousand dollars to kill cach enemy soldier, while we spend only fifty-three dollars for each person classified as poor." This is indeed troubling and highlights the fact that the poor are miserably neglected compared to the cost of foreign wars and armaments.

Bergner (2005) cited the need for church leaders to call for action on poverty based on a statement by Jim Wallis, leader and director of Sojourners:

> Mr. Wallis called the daily death of 30,000 children due to poverty- related causes a "silent tsunami" and pointed out that the yearly subsidy of an English cow is greater than the yearly income of most Africans. "Poverty is the new slavery."

While this comment referred to international concerns, the danger and hardship of those in poverty is akin to slavery. Poverty among African Americans is a compounded scenario given the hardships and oppressions endured.

Thurow (1969) noted the complexities of poverty among African Americans and their struggle to emerge from it. Clearly, racial discrimination is a significant factor.

> Investigations of poverty reveal that racial discrimination is an important factor. Much of the poverty suffered by blacks can be ascribed to discrimination in one of its many forms. Thus programs designed to eliminate white poverty will not eliminate black poverty. Nor will the elimination of racial discrimination solve the problem of poverty. Discrimination and poverty are as intertwined as Siamese twins: they need two policies, one to fight the causes of poverty and another to reduce discrimination. (p. 1)

African Americans endured and continue to endure the hardships of both poverty and the footprints of generational indignity.

Barack Obama (2006), the first African American President of the United States, wrote that there is a volatile issue that undermines progress and worsens relations in the African American community: that issue "is the deteriorating condition of the inner-city poor" (p. 249).

African Americans view poverty and repression as

acutely familiar in their lives. Neither of which is soon to be eliminated.

Stricker (2007) explains how poverty has been viewed over many years:

> Two hundred years ago, poverty was a pressing issue in the United States . . . In those years, as in other times, the causes of poverty were debated, but most people chose one of two big explanations. The first blamed the poor; laziness or foolishness caused them to be impoverished. The second emphasized political and economic structures that failed to provide enough jobs and that dealt too much income to the rich and too little to the majority. (p. 1)

Harrington wrote a book that became popular in debates on poverty. Frank Stricker (2007) observes,

> Harrington simply followed common practice by describing the links between poverty and such social handicaps as inadequate education, old age, work in a low-wage industry, broken families, and racial background." Stricker adds that this "emphasis was both accurate and misleading . . . (Did broken families cause poverty or vice versa?) (p. 45).

Stricker asserts that Harrington divided the poor (which included many African Americans) into two groups, the poor and those who are not so poor. Stricker submitted that Harrington made it appear as if their problems differed, even politically separating the two groups. The idea of a "culture of poverty" developed, suggesting a cyclical, sick environment as the reason for poverty. Stricker (2007) submits Harrington sees the poor in a "different mental world, a culture of poverty" (p. 45).

Stricker continues with the record of Harrington's own words, when he says the poor "should be defined psychologically . . . [as] internal exiles who, almost inevitably, develop attitudes of defeat and pessimism and who are therefore excluded from taking advantage of new opportunities" (p. 45).

Oscar Lewis is credited with coming up with the term "culture of poverty." An article from *Time Books: Culture of Poverty* (n.d.) explains the difference between poverty and the "culture of poverty."

> Lewis draws a distinction between poverty and what he calls the "culture of poverty"—a perpetuation, at society's lowest levels, of the patterns of life that form, over generations and sometimes centuries, a kind of prison. It is a prison whose door stands open a crack, says Lewis, but it is also one from which the inmates do not readily escape: "It is much more difficult to eliminate the culture of poverty than to eliminate poverty per se."

Although Lewis is not seen as "blaming the victim" by some, Philen (2007) states, "It involved recognizing that poverty doesn't entail simply not having enough money, but also often entails the necessity for adaptive strategies for dealing with persistent poverty."

Crutchfield and Pettinicchio (2009, 623:135) detail a penetrating assessment that is very different from a "culture of poverty." It is a "taste of inequalities." Crutchfield and Pettinicchio state that there is an increasing "taste of inequality" that stands against the idea of the "culture of poverty" argument.

They contend a "number of social problems are produced by persistent poverty, which exists not because of perverted values among the poor, but rather because of values in the larger society that are accepting of social inequality" (p. 135). Critchfield and Pettinicchio further state:

> This culture of inequality reaches its highest form among modern-day social Darwinists who believe that the problems of the poor, the unemployed, and the uneducated are due to their own failures. This view holds that the government intervention to help these groups will lead to further dependency. Such efforts, according to the argument, only waste the money of hard working taxpayers. (p. 135)

These modern-day social Darwinists in essence see the problems of the poor as a case of the "survival of the fittest." It assumes the problems stem from the poor themselves, as ignorant, lazy, and just plain failures.

Crutchfield and Pettinicchio would disagree with these Darwinists. They contend the "taste of inequality" is the observable manifestation of the presence of a culture of inequality. The former is the operationalization of the latter (pp. 135, 136). In essence, the "taste of inequality" keeps the "culture of inequality" operating in society.

Crutchfield and Pettinicchio also cited that there are more prisoners in the United States prison system than 14 other countries combined; this is a blatant example of the taste of inequalities. Where that taste becomes broadly accepted among the citizenry, a culture of inequality is likely to invest less in social welfare and to respond more punitively to crime. Of particular interest is how the United States, which has had unprecedented increases in imprisonment as well as cutbacks in welfare programs, compares to other nations (p. 136).

More money is spent on prison systems and social controls, which call for increases in budget, while the social welfare of citizens is reduced. The implication is that revenue for prisons would be better spent uplifting those in persistent poverty rather than needless incarcerations; for certain many

The old Tennessee State Prison operated from 1898–1992. It admitted 1,403 prisoners to its 800 cells on its first day of operation. The former prison has been the filming site of multiple movies, including Green Mile, Last Castle, and Walk the Line.

incarcerations could have be prevented if the "taste of inequalities" did not exist in society against African Americans, Latinos, and other people of color.

When it comes to incarcerations, Crutchfield and Pettinicchio say the United States has 1,208,711 prisoners. This was more than Austria, Belgium, Canada, Finland, France, Great Britain, Germany, Iceland, Ireland, Italy, Netherlands, Norway, Spain, and Sweden combined (p. 140).

Crutchfield and Pettinicchio show how this impacts dignity:

> During the post-Great Society years, and especially since the election of Ronald Reagan, the United States has experienced widespread, pop-

ular acceptance of culture of inequality values ... As a result of this increase in the collective tastes for inequality, racial injustice is essentially reduced to a historical fact with little or no bearing on contemporary life chances of people of color. Thus, affirmative action is now defined as discrimination against the privileged. (pp. 136, 137)

Crutchfield and Pettinicchio further state the "taste of inequality" impacts incarceration, how crime is viewed, and how politicians may run for office based on this taste.

Most crime is viewed as a consequence of rational choices by people unable or unwilling to defer gratification. In turn, society responds harshly to punish offenders and to deter the "not-yet-detected" ... From 1973 to 1997, incarceration numbers in the United States increased fivefold ... is explained in part by a growing taste of inequality as well as politicians' willingness to run for office on platforms that pander to the view that substantial inequality is acceptable and even just." (p. 137)

The connection to incarceration should be obvious. Needless to say, incarcerations bring a strain on families and family incomes that are devastating. More will be said about this problem later.

With the breakup of homes, children grow up without their father or mother, either way the income is reduced and social adjustments for children becomes troubling.

74

In an article titled "Prison Population Exceeds Two Million" (n.d.) the numbers illustrate an alarming connection in this manner.

> About 10.4% of the entire African-American male population in the United States aged 25 to 29 was incarcerated, by far the largest racial or ethnic group—by comparison, 2.4% of Hispanic men and 1.2% of white men in that same age group were incarcerated. According to a report by the Justice Policy Institute in 2002, the number of black men in prison has grown to five times the rate it was twenty years ago. Today, more African-American men are in jail than in college. In 2000 there were 791,600 black men in prison and 603,032 enrolled in college. In 1980, there were 143,000 black men in prison and 463,700 enrolled in college.

The burden of incarcerations is similar to slavery. Prisoners become captives of indignity. They are trafficked in their own country and enslaved in prisons built for profit. They suffer as enslaved prisoners, prohibited from employment, opportunities, and human justice. They become disheartened, discriminated against, and demoralized.

Martineau (2008) writes about a flawed approach to crime and punishment in the United States and says,

> The United States has less than 5 percent of the world's population. But it has almost a quarter of the world's prisoners. Indeed, the United

States leads the world in producing prisoners, a reflection of a relatively recent and now entirely distinctive American approach to crime and punishment. Americans are locked up for crimes — from writing bad checks to using drugs — that would rarely produce prison sentences in other countries. And in particular they are kept incarcerated far longer than prisoners in other nations. Criminologists and legal scholars in other industrialized nations say they are mystified and appalled by the number and length of American prison sentences.

China has four times the population of United States, but the number of those incarcerated is greater than China, and a disproportionate number of African Americans are incarcerated. Thus, many poor African Americans and others have met their demise on the "plantations" of incarceration.

African Americans often faced poor legal representation, which resulted in their imprisonment as well as inadequate resources. Others were later found to be innocent of charges they faced through DNA testing. Those living in the poorest communities need fair and equal justice, avoiding the criminalization based on ethnicity and the lack of resources.

When individuals are released from prison it is difficult for them to find employment. Poverty once again is a negative accompaniment to a lack of dignity. Crutchfield and Pettinicchio's assessment of the "taste of inequalities" show validity that African Americans' are not yet equivalent to some in society.

The uphill journey for African Americans is underscored by research conducted and funded by a grant from the U.S. Department of Agriculture, Cornell's New York State Agricultural Experiment Station in Ithaca, and Federal Hatch. Friedlander (1999) revealed a stunning statistic about African Americans and poverty: "more than 90 percent will have lived below the poverty line by age 75." Quoted within the same news article, the research cites the alarming fact "that virtually every [Black] American will experience poverty at some point during their adulthood."

All of the struggles along the way can be summed up as struggles for human dignity and human rights. African Americans sought dignity while in slavery, through the constitution, through discrimination, the Civil War, codes, laws, the Supreme Court, local courts, and poverty.

These impoverished neighborhoods are the result of years of mistreatment, disproportionate incarcerations, oppression, and lack of opportunities. Pressed down and exploited, through ignorance and misunderstandings, African Americans were seen as inferior and incapable by many in society.

These undesirable experiences of African Americans' and poverty are related. It also led some to an improper assessment of personhood due to these experiences. Barack Obama (2006) the 44th President of the United States, sums up the history and personal stories of many African Americans and the effects and experiences of the poor living in neighborhoods of poverty:

> These are the stories of those who didn't make it out of history's confinement, of the neighborhoods within the black community that house the poorest of the poor, serving as repositories for all the scars of slavery and violence of Jim Crow, the internalized rage and the forced ignorance, the sham of men who could not protect their women or support their families, the children who grew up being told they wouldn't amount to anything and had no one there to undo the damage. (p. 252)

Who are they who make the policies? What is the approach of law enforcement and incarcerations in the neighborhood community? Who are those who are the less than in financial resources? What can be done to improve policies, law enforcement, reduction of unlawful incarcerations and poverty towards dignity for all?

Therefore, when it comes to African Americans, Freeman (1998) suggests "researchers and policy makers need to better understand such questions as: What have been the consequences of certain historical periods of African American experiences and how have these experiences shaped their contemporary experiences?"

CHAPTER 6

THE SUPPRESSION OF RESOURCES

The issue of poverty among African Americans includes the lack of resources for living; it also consists of past and present deliberate dehumanization, and suppression. *A misconception of poverty is the notion that those of poverty are lazy, not wanting nor willing to work.* However, during slavery, enslaved Africans did the most work, but they were the most impoverished. Cleaning, ironing, yard work, fieldwork, later motel/hotel work, railroads, mining, janitorial, and other physical jobs were available to them.

Later, government programs meant to assist whites were rarely available for blacks. *The notion that someone pulled him/herself up by their own bootstraps is rarely the truth. Inheritances gained from others and privilege played a much larger roll than pulling straps on one's boots.*

There is a seventeen-minute video on YouTube detailing how deliberate suppression of resources occurred, by Phil Pascher retrieved September 10, 2020, https://www.youtube.

com/watch?v=AGUwcs9qJXY. The video will answer many questions about poverty in the African American community and how it happened. It is recommended viewing before reading the rest of this chapter.

This chapter will review the impact of the past as it continues to resonate through systems, structures and expressions of hurting human hearts.

The information listed below, showing poverty from government sources, is an actual example of statistics and figures between 2008 through June 2009. These figures would be outdated today but serve as a good example of a recession. It also indicates financial poverty levels of individuals and families.

The U.S. Census Bureau of 2009 establishes poverty thresholds by family size and income. It determines the maximums of income and family sizes as measures of meeting that threshold. These measures are for statistical purposes, understanding people, ethnic groups, households, and regions.

A United States Census Bureau Report (2009) provides poverty thresholds for poverty incomes and family households and are listed in this manner: one person $10,956; two persons $13,991; three persons $17,098; four persons $21,954; five persons $25,991; six persons $29,405; seven persons $33,752; eight persons $37,252; and nine persons

$44,366. However, families with incomes below $25,000 are generally considered to be at the poverty level.

The "Federal Poverty Guidelines" (2009), is different, and establishes poverty ranges to determine financial aid services by income and family size. Many times, aid is in the form of food vouchers so the poor can eat. This government source provides poverty guidelines and family household sizes to indicate those of poverty. They are listed in this manner: one person $10,830; two persons $14,570; three persons $18,310; four persons $22,050; five persons $25,790; six persons $29,530; seven persons $33,270; eight persons $38,010; and $3,740 is added to each additional person, thereby making nine persons in a household $41,750 dollars.

While the starting and ending figures for determining poverty by Census thresholds and Federal Poverty Guidelines differ, they are similar; in fact, they overlap each other at times.

What the figures do not reveal are the circumstances that led to poverty nor the compensation. Some circumstances affecting poverty are lack of employment, the inability to finish high school, illness or some other malady. While difficulties assail humankind, African Americans consistently experience poverty in higher percentages.

It is noted that the U.S. Census (revised May 2012) indicates in "2010, 46. 2 million people were in poverty." The same source stated, "between 2009 and 2010, the poverty rate increased for Whites (from 9.4 percent to 9.9 percent), for Blacks (from 25.8 percent to 27.4 percent), and for Hispanics (from 25.3 percent to 26.6 percent)" Asians remained at 12.1 percent.

Below are some facts that identify the financial difficulties African Americans had to face and continue to experience.

- The starting block of African ancestry was that their distant predecessors were slaves (uncompensated).

- They lived and worked on plantations.

- After slavery African Americans had nowhere to go since they did not own the (crude shanty) homes they lived in.

- After slavery many ended up working as sharecroppers for the same people they worked for as slaves.

- African Americans still lack home ownership. This is one of the best ways to leave an inheritance to children. In the past Blacks could not live in every community, nor could they get the financing to do so. "Redlining— red marks on maps that loan corporations would use to outline mixed-race or African American neighborhoods. Neighborhoods in more-affluent areas, which were deemed the most worthy of loans, were usually outlined in blue or green." (https://www.britannica. com/topic/redlining)

• The idea that African Americans needed to pull up their bootstraps suggested that they needed to work harder. They worked from sun up 'til sun down. It was not the lack of work - it was the lack of pay.

• African American families still have only a fraction of the wealth of white families and fewer opportunities for economic progress because of discrimination.

• African Americans still find it difficult to find steady jobs. There is also a lack of available jobs that pay good wages even with a good education.

African slaves were denied the right to an education, which was supported by unjust laws, as noted earlier. The enormous impact of those decisions and other denials still has ramifications in the lives of African Americans today.

Educational difficulties increase when there are issues and challenges of poverty, such as: health issues, nourishing diets, adequate tools for learning like computers, books, and sufficient educational facilities.

Winters and Greene (2002) report,

> The national graduation rate for the public school class of 2000 was 69%. The rate for white students was 76%; for Asian students it was 79%; for African-Americans it was 55%; for Hispanic students it was 53%; and for Native Americans it was 57%.

Did poverty play a factor in these percentages? Was dignity wounded? The answers to these questions cannot be answered with any certainty; however, given the historical past, which affects the present, it is probable.

Depending on the year of the statistics, more African Americans tend to be affected. In addition, it is basically employment-generated funds that sustain a family. Inheritances from parents, grandparents, and/or previous family members in the African American communities are scarce.

Weiss (2009), reporting on economic security for unmarried women, states,

> More than one in five (22.2 percent) women living in poverty are elderly women age 60 and older. Losing a husband to death or divorce can be devastating to women's quality of life and greatly increases risk of poverty. Because the vast majority (95 percent) of today's elderly population has married at some point, older women who are poor are almost all previously married. The new Census figures bear this out. Widows accounted for nearly half (45.6 percent) of poor women age 60 and older in 2008, and 65 percent of those over 75. An additional one-quarter (23.5 percent) of poor women 60 and over were divorced or separated. By the end of their lives, nearly all poor elderly women age 75 and older are on their own—more than 80 percent of poor women this age are unmarried and more than three-quarters of these live alone.

When there are families where the husband and the wife are working, poverty is usually reduced. The fact is, however, when it comes to poverty, single households comprise a greater percentage of poverty than married households. Weiss (2009) states,

> Women are more likely even in better economic times to face poverty than men, and unmarried women have higher poverty rates than married women. Yet the marital disparity has worsened since early in the decade. The poverty rate of unmarried women was 13.4 percentage points higher than married women in 2000, but it was 14.6 percentage points higher in 2008. The risk of poverty for women of color is even greater, especially for those who are unmarried. Thirty percent of unmarried black women and 29.5 percent of unmarried Hispanic women—of any race— were poor in 2008, compared with 18.5 percent of unmarried white women.

The history of home ownership for slaves was essentially non-existent. Those who held them as slaves owned them and the homes they lived in. One of the ways to advance with dignity and create a heritage for one's family is home ownership.

In "Conditions of Antebellum Slavery" (n.d.), the homes slaves lived in are described like this: "They lived in crude quarters that left them vulnerable to bad weather and disease. Their clothing and bedding were minimal as well."

Slaves had little rights to owning property especially in the South for they themselves were considered property.

Kelly, Baker, O'Donovan, and Brown, in "After Slavery" (n.d.) inform us that

> freed people continued to work under their former owners for nominal wages that made little real difference in their material well-being. ... Planters reacted with bitterness to the new 'free labor' arrangements by casting them out of their former homes, leaving the most vulnerable to patch together a bare subsistence as best they could, or to die in hunger and squalor.

A study of African American home ownership in southwestern Pennsylvania revealed an interesting finding. Home ownership rates for African Americans in cities "that are more residentially segregated tend to have higher African American ownership rates" ("The Reinvestment Fund," 2004, p. 9). The city of Birmingham, which is racially segregated, has an African American ownership of 51.76 percent (p. 36).

This is encouraging in one sense, for a little over half of African Americans own their home, which is higher than many other cities. However, further study reveals it is low compared to Whites, the same source says the median home value was $62,200 for African Americans in Birmingham (p. 36). This median home value was in the top five of the lowest

103 cities cited. Therefore, many homes were purchased in concentrated poor neighborhoods.

When one considers net worth in finance, one's home is a major part of that net worth. The saying "location, location, location" in the realty business relates to the value of your home and where it is located. That value can mean the difference between home value going up or down.

Again, a home is usually the largest investment one will ever make. African Americans, who rent from others all their lives, pass on little in the form of financial net worth to their family, continuing a cycle of poverty for generations.

An article titled "African Americans: The State of the Disparity" (n.d.) shows the disparity and enormity of the problem.

> When African Americans do buy homes, they receive the highest interest mortgage loans 30% more often than whites, even when their incomes and credit scores are the same. This differential in lending terms cumulatively costs African American homeowners more than $6 billion dollars each year. (p. 2)

Another disparity of net worth written by Blue (2008),

> And anybody who's paying any attention to what's going on in America today understands, if you are African-American in this country today,

you are likely to have a net worth of about 10 percent of what white families have.

The purchasing of homes can boost one's net worth, and one's net worth can boost a greater standard of living. Blue agrees, when she states:

> Net worth is measured as the total value of a household's financial assets—such as bank accounts, property and vehicles—minus the household's financial liabilities. Though the measurement is an oft-used indicator of financial health, it doesn't always tell the whole story because the amount of income generated by a household's assets is a key factor in maintaining a desired standard of living. (2008)

Starling (1998) informs us that the top ten diseases that kill African Americans are heart disease, cancer, accidents, strokes, homicides, aids, diabetes, pneumonia/influenza, asthma/bronchitis, and infant mortality.

Starling (1998) stresses that the same diseases affect Whites as well. Furthermore, she states, "by the time most Blacks are diagnosed with these illnesses, they are more likely to die ... With regular checkups and simple changes in lifestyle and nutrition, many of these health threats can be avoided."

Daniels, (as cited in Starling, 1998) referring to African Americans, said, "Most patients still feel that to go to the doctor, something has to be wrong," but for some it is too late to reverse the problem. Another doctor suggests, "a lot of confusion is due to a legacy of racism by the medical community and poverty in Black America."

In the medical arena, it is well known now that many African Americans viewed White doctors and medical institutions with suspicion, especially after they were targeted with deception according to the Center for Disease Control and Prevention (n.d.) in the "Tuskegee Study of Untreated Syphilis in the "Negro male."

African Americans thought they were being treated for the disease; they were unaware that they were given medications that were useless from 1932–1972. The adverse effect of this experience for many African Americans has been a reluctance to receive medical healings. This unfortunate decision, however, is devastating to the prevention and cure of diseases among African Americans.

One of the problems for the poor is not having enough money to pay for expensive medicines. Some choose not to have their prescriptions filled, making tough decisions between medicine and other expenses.

Bromley (2010) explains obesity and poverty,

> People living near, at or below "poverty level"
> tend to be at higher risk for obesity and the health
> issues that come with it. There is a good reason

for that; these folks can't afford to eat healthy even though they may know what good health habits, and healthy eating habits really are. Most do not eat well balanced meals and do not live healthy lifestyles. The two go hand in hand. Unhealthy diets lead to obesity and other health issues. Among these issues are heart disease, kidney disease, cancers, respiratory problems, joint and muscle diseases as well as learning disabilities and a variety of psychological disorders.

It has been said that all work has dignity; many African Americans did not have an opportunity to decide where they worked, for they were kept away from the significant positions of labor. Domestic workers, on the other hand, worked on the land and cleaned houses in many neighborhoods not in the community where they lived, therefore receiving low wages generally given and assigned to African Americans.

In an abstract, Donavan (1987) details how the health care industry is becoming one of the dominant places of employment for domestic workers.

The home health care industry is emerging as a significant employer of low income for minorities in the United States. Many of the new nonprofessional jobs, such as home attendant and home health aide, are structured within subemployment systems that keep wages low and benefits few or nonexistent. The conditions have historical roots in U.S. slavery and the persistent segregation of black women in work roles as domestic servants in private households.

Consequently, many minority children today who dream of distancing themselves from the legacy of domestic work (which is the legacy of compulsory slavery), find themselves instead with low-income nonprofessional jobs.

Many African American children have seen their parents labor as domestic workers. It sometimes stirs a desire in them to choose a different course.

When it comes to money and receiving government assistance, one must meet the criteria of poverty. For those who receive assistance, a certain amount of humility and indignity comes with it.

Food assistance is available to those who qualify. According to "Social Security Online" (n.d.), "federal, state and local governments provide many programs designed to help meet the nutritional needs of people with low incomes and their families." Those available according to the same source are,

> Food Stamp Programs; Special Supplemental Nutrition Program for Women, Infants and Children (WIC); Nutrition Services Incentive Program (NSIP) [for elderly people]; The Child and Adult Care Food Program offers meals and snacks to children in eligible day care centers; The School Lunch and Breakfast Programs offer meals at schools to children. Low-income children get

these meals free or at a reduced price; The Summer Food Service Program offers free meals and snacks to needy children during the months when school is not in session; The Senior Farmers' Market Nutrition Program provides low-income seniors (individuals who are at least 60 years old) with coupons during the harvest season that can be exchanged for eligible foods at farmers' markets, roadside stands and community supported agriculture programs.

According to Plotkin (2009),

> a new report released this week by Washington University in St. Louis researchers found that 90 percent of black children will be clients of the national Supplemental Nutrition Assistance Program (SNAP/Food Stamps) at least once by the time they turn 20.

The above quote stresses that this should be a time when a child is experiencing a sense of safety and security; instead, it is a time of economic turmoil. Economic turmoil in turn adds physical, mental, and emotional stress in the home.

The burden becomes greater for African American singles. Plotkin (2009) says,

> Ninety-one percent of children with single parents will be in a household receiving food stamps, compared to 37 percent of children in married households. Looking at race, marital status and

education simultaneously, children who are black
and whose head of household is not married with
less than 12 years of education have a cumulative
percentage of residing in a food stamp household
of 97 percent by age 10.

It should not be surprising that percentage wise many African Americans are in poverty and need assistance. What may be still surprising to some is that it is Whites, and not Blacks that benefit from government services the most.

Marguerite Ward (2020) writes, "In fact, far more white people have benefited from US welfare programs over the years—reflecting their greater share of the population— while Black people and other people of color have been denied them in various ways . . ."

Again, the wealth gap has grown wider over the years due in part to the changing of laws and federal government policies, as well as other adverse factors affecting people of color, such as the impact of slavery.

Varshney (2002) though not speaking to the experience of African Americans, his words are few but they sum up and bridge the impact of poverty and dignity when he writes, "Both poverty and the denial of dignity together constitute a more serious force . . . than poverty alone" (p. 23).

CHAPTER 7

PRELUDE TO KILLING
MOCKINGBIRDS

When one lives in poverty, coping skills are needed to survive. Adjustments to daily circumstances and depending on others are part of surviving poverty. Individuals living in poverty rely on others to spread the word about where they can find help to survive. However, no amount of coping skills will suffice against deep pain and fatal tragedies that assail communities of color. *This chapter will detail some of those fatal tragedies and adjustments which emerged from assumed crimes and trivial notions, so inconsequential but disastrously led (and still lead) to death. These assumed crimes by people of color, complicated by poverty, seldom occur in affluent white neighborhoods.*

Some adjustments of those in poverty include paying to get checks cashed because they generally don't have bank accounts, the giving of blood at a blood bank for money, and turning in a car for a title loan. Those in poverty have difficult times maintaining mortgage payments, or paying rent, and often their car becomes their largest investment. Cars are traded in for exorbitant fees through high interest rates, which inflame an already exacerbated situation of poverty.

Neiger (2008) reveals how much interest one could pay when making title loans:

> Car title lenders are in a different category than credit card companies or banks and work around usury laws. Thus, title loan lenders are able to charge triple digit annual percentage rates (APRs). Yes, triple digits. It's not an exaggeration to see 250% APR and higher on these car tile loans and only a handful of states have passed strict laws that prohibit exorbitant percentage rates.

By using elevated interest rates title loan companies are not really benefiting the customer. Instead, they use the plight of the poor for the companies benefit. Neiger (2008) explains their intentions:

> The terms of these loans are crafted to keep bor- rowers in a cycle of debt and bring customers either to the verge of repossession or to actual repossession. Not being able to pay off the initial loan and then renewing it the next month costs borrowers even more money in interest, on top of the original amount they've already borrowed.

Image taken by Dr. Gaiter
A storefront like many title loans and advance cash businesses.

These types of loans are made to people who are already strapped for cash, and are most often made in emergency situations. Quite often the time allotted to pay back these loans are longer/shorter, and costlier than the borrower expects. Title loans sometimes leave many customers in a place where they will not be able to redeem their merchandise.

The use of pawnshops are also utilized as an adjustment to the difficulties of poverty. Slowly all the assets that one possesses become the assets of another, and one's net worth is reduced to a lower degree.

Pawnshops are favorite places to obtain immediate cash because of their ability to receive a variety of goods in exchange for money. However, the interest rates are high and the loan to value of one's merchandise is low.

Morrissey (2010) shares these comments,

> Pawnshop companies make money by giving short-term loans to customers who offer jewelry, electronics, tools, musical instruments and other merchandise as collateral or by purchasing merchandise outright from customers at a steep discount. Loan terms are typically one to three months in length, with customers expected to cough up monthly storage and loan-servicing fees of 10% to 20% a month. If a customer fails to make a monthly payment, the pawnshop, following a grace period, can sell the item.

In addition to pawnshops, the above article addresses payday loans. These are working salary loans given in advance of normal payment to those in need. These loans are

> short-term loans, typically seven to 30 days in length, that are not backed by merchandise. The loans typically carry interest rates of 10% to 20% for a two-week term, which translates into an annual percentage rate exceeding 300%. Industry experts say the APR is just theoretical since payday loans are meant to be very short term, lasting only until the borrower's next paycheck. Even so, a number of states, like Ohio, are imposing caps on the rates in an effort to stop what they consider to be predatory lending.

Large banks are now presenting payday loans to their customers. Choi (2011) notes,

> Banks say their loans are intended for emergencies and are quick to distance themselves from the payday lending industry. But consumer advocates say these direct deposit loans, as banks prefer to call them, bear the same predatory trademarks as the payday loans commonly found in low-income neighborhoods.

Choi suggests that though the fees are smaller, they are still high. To assure that the banks receive their money, the loan must be paid back through direct deposit.

Desperate measures are seen by the frequent use of advanced money systems. When a person looks at the availability of these systems in any city, what one will discover is that these systems thrive in poorer areas and near military bases.

While it does not necessarily mean that all the persons using advanced money systems are those at poverty levels, it does indicate there is likely to be desperation for money from those living in those areas. A factor for using these systems could simply be that individuals are overly extended in debt rather than poverty.

While people in poverty use these systems, those whose incomes are not at the poverty level are customers as well according to the findings. Persons on social security whose checks arrive once a month are also likely customers.

African slaves and their ancestry constantly sang songs which expressed a hopeful future in their life adjustments such as "Swing Low, Sweet Chariot," "There Is a Balm in Gilead," "Deep River," and others. African American parents often expressed a 'better day' theme to their children who watched them washing and ironing someone else's clothes, and cleaning someone else's home, then arriving at their own home physically tired, and emotionally belittled, looking for a better day.

Learning to cope in poverty is a must. Habits and adjustments become patterns, which leaves those of poverty sometimes in a vicious circle. The downside of some adjustments veer toward alcohol and drug use, and other maladjustments of social life. Those in poverty at times can be both participants in and victims of crime. As a consequence, those who live in poverty and crime saturated areas not only look for a better day in the future, they look for a 'better day' in the present.

According to Goffman (1956), embarrassment or being flustered is "considered evidence of weakness, inferiority, low status, moral guilt, defeat, and other unenviable attributes" (p. 266).

What is significant about these attributes is that they also encircle meanings that describe the lack of dignity. According to the same source, embarrassment "occurs whenever an individual is felt to have projected incompatible definitions of himself before those present" (p. 264).

Goffman (1956) contends that dignity of a "social encounter" and its makeup "then consist of effectively projecting claims to an acceptable self and the confirmation of like claims on the part of others. The contributions of all are oriented to these and built upon the basis of them" (p. 268).

Many African Americans face insufficiency in its full brunt. This becomes evident as they look at the unleveled playing field in a wide area of opportunities that leads to prisons of embarrassment and undeveloped dignity.

This may explain why some African Americans withdraw in the face of difficulty, sensing the history of a different set of laws and a different kind of treatment. The full weight of "somebodyness" is absent.

Taylor (2010) expresses how African Americans navigated ways to travel without embarrassment in the 1930s.

> The Negro Motorist Green Book was a publication released in 1936 that served as a guide for African American travelers. Because of the racist conditions that existed from segregation, blacks needed a reference manual to guide them to integrated or black-friendly establishments ... originally provided to serve Metropolitan New York, the book received such an alarming response, it was spread throughout the country within one year. The catch phrase was "Now we can travel without embarrassment."

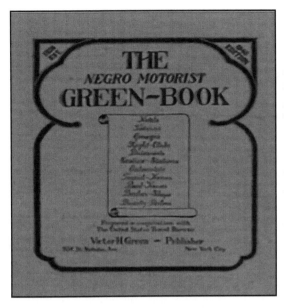

Retrieved from history.com **This book listed safe places to eat, sleep, and travel in Jim Crow days.**

Having an automobile was important to African Americans. It gave a sense of freedom without having to be discriminated against when traveling by train, and other means of transportation. <u>The Green Book</u> gave a list of hotels where African Americans could stay overnight. There were certain restaurants that refused to serve them just because of the color of their skin. <u>The Green Book </u>was an important resource that provided the names of places where they could go without the fear of being embarrassed, harassed, or denied service.

Being ashamed can be personal, yet it can hinge on others. Allison (2009) quotes fourth and fifth graders on the relationship of poverty and learning:

> That children who live in poverty ... say that poverty is "feeling ashamed when my dad can't get

a job, pretending that you forgot your lunch, not buying books at the book fair" and "not getting to go on school trips." Poverty is detrimental to student health and exclusion seriously undermines low-income students' confidence.

Ashamedness involves a circle of circumstances, pretending to give a defense for and compensate for what one does not have, and the inability to participate on a normal level as others.

Those who are in positions of responsibility must transcend what dehumanizes and causes undue embarrassment and ashamedness on others, depriving them of dignity.

African Americans have known and experienced what it means to be socially excluded. The act of exclusion according to a previous quote undermines confidence. Steele (1992) highlights how confidence is undermined.

> More than half of black college students fail to complete their degree work—for reasons that have little to do with innate ability or environmental conditioning. The problem, a social psychologist argues, is that they are undervalued, in ways that are sometimes subtle and sometimes not.

The undervaluedness of Black college students is subtle, and erodes meaning in life. The confidences which can be found by interacting with others in educational arenas are important to achievement and important to life itself.

103

Stillman, Baumeister, Lambert, Crescioni, DeWall, and Fincham (2009) confirm this threat of erosion when they say, "social exclusion could threaten people at such a basic level that it would impair their sense of meaningful existence."

While changes in laws and institutions are slow to create a climate of inclusion, those who understand the problem can visualize dignity as a start toward meaningful relationships.

There are other difficulties of life than poverty. In fact, some see discussing poverty of income as a narrow way of looking at insufficiency. This book does not deny that the traditional view of poverty is a lack of income, it includes aspects of emotional, mental, spiritual, and social poverty in the life experiences of African Americans.

Davis (n.d.) gives excellent definitions of other levels of poverty, which he believes should be considered, such as emotional poverty.

> A person experiences emotional poverty when they have endured a traumatic experience that has so scarred them emotionally that they lack the ability to achieve emotional balance. Too, a person may have endured a harsh childhood or some other harsh environment that caused their emotional maturity to be stunted.

Another deficit of poverty is mental poverty. Davis shares how someone can have mental poverty.

Mental poverty can come from a variety of sources such as lack of proper education, abuse, constantly being put down, etc. These individuals have learned to deal with these unfortunate realities in their life by compensating in a way they only knew how. They are not mentally ill, in that their habits are due to a dysfunction mentally, but rather they are mentally poor due to a lack of knowing how to mentally deal with their reality ... Those who find themselves in this situation should take hope that they can overcome their mental struggles, whether it is extreme anxiety, extreme moods, etc.

Davis also addresses spiritual poverty. He stresses the need for people to be connected to God.

Many find themselves spiritually poor. Spiritual poverty occurs when a person lacks a connection with God and feels as though they are alone in this life with no true purpose or hope beyond the here and now. Too, a person can be spiritually poor, though they have a relationship with God. This person may have been hurt by religion, the church or in some other way. They may still seek God, but feel so hurt that they just float aimlessly trying to find their way.

Another poverty listed by Davis is social poverty. Those who lack the ability to have relationships with others amounts to poverty.

Social poverty occurs when a person lacks the

ability to have whole relationships with others. Either they have not been taught how relationships work or they have developed certain habits that drive others away. Some have only been in bad relationships. These individuals lack the vision of what a good relationship looks like.

So, when poverty is considered, according to de Oliveira and Duraiappah (n.d.) the human well-being must be taken into consideration.

> Human well-being is therefore about the expansion of human capabilities—the ability to achieve what individuals have reason to value. Poverty is the pronounced deprivation of human well-being or in other words the pronounced deprivation of human capabilities.

How poverty interferes with achievement in developing countries is chronicled in an UNICEF article (n.d.) that leaves little doubt about the impact of poverty on achievement.

> Poverty contributes to malnutrition, which in turn is a contributing factor in over half of the under-five deaths in developing countries ... The best start in life is critical in a child's first few years, not only to survival but to her or his physical, intellectual and emotional development. So these deprivations greatly hamper children's ability to achieve their full potential, contributing to a society's cycle of endless poverty and hunger.

Achievement is considered as one of the necessary attributes of dignity. Therefore, when dignity is considered through the eyes of poverty, human well-being can be deprived of capabilities that would ordinarily present themselves in achievements.

Earlier the subject of discrimination was addressed in this book regarding African Americans and dignity. It is important to address it again.

Discrimination denies opportunity and allows poverty to flourish. Together they prevent the ability to perform. Discrimination separates those who can from those who cannot often based on what one has or does not have. Harsher punishment is given to those who cannot defend themselves. Unconscionable guiltiness is rendered based on appearance. An African American would be viewed guilty or suspicious because of skin color or clothing worn, or what cannot be defended.

Bryan Stevenson (2014) penned in his book *Just Mercy*.

> I've come to believe that the true measure of our commitment to justice, the character of our society, our commitment to the rule of law, fairness, and equality cannot be measured by how we treat the rich, the powerful, the privileged, and the respected among us. The true measure of our character is how we treat the poor, the disfavored, the accused, the incarcerated, and the condemned.

A young man who worked selling vegetables on behalf of his family started a wave of protest in Tunisia. When denied basic rights to make a living his actions spearheaded protest in Tunisia and across other areas in the Middle East. Abouzeid (2011) reveals,

> Mohammed Bouazizi never set out to be a byword . . . But on Dec. 17 his livelihood was threatened when a policewoman confiscated his unlicensed vegetable cart and its goods. It wasn't the first time it had happened, but it would be the last. At 11:30 a.m., less than an hour after the confrontation with the policewoman and without telling his family, Bouazizi returned to the elegant double-story white building with arched azure shutters, poured fuel over himself and set himself on fire. He did not die right away but lingered in the hospital till Jan. 4. There was so much outrage over his ordeal that even President Zine el Abidine Ben Ali, the dictator, visited Bouazizi on Dec. 28 to try to blunt the anger. But the outcry could not be suppressed and, on Jan. 14, just 10 days after Bouazizi died, Ben Ali's 23-year rule of Tunisia was over. Though proud of the consequences of Bouazizi's self-immolation, his family is still indescribably sad. "Mohammed did what he did for the sake of his dignity," says his mother, Mannoubia.

Mohammed's expression against needless restraint, the need to provide for his family, and indignity was more than he could bear.

It is repeated hundreds of times with African Americans. A person's life is taken because of assumed suspicious notions about African Americans.

There are many perils that African Americans are confronted with, children included. The failure to regard them with dignity has resulted in their experiencing the following preludes to death at higher rates:
- African Americans are more likely to be imprisoned.
- African Americans experience health care disparities at alarmingly high rates, and live in food deserts.
- Environmental issues such as lead, chemical poisoning, and toxic waste are more prevalent in their communities.
- African Americans are far more likely to face death at the hand police shootings over minor infractions.
- African American parents have to have "The Talk" with their son/s and daughter/s.

To Kill A Mockingbird, a well-known book written by Harper Lee is a story of innocence being destroyed. *There are thousands of innocent African Americans who have been killed because of erroneous notions since slavery.*

Listed below are a few names of individuals who have recently needlessly, innocently died.
- 17-year-old Trayvon Martin (followed)
- Amadou Diallo (mistaken rape suspect shot at 40 times)
- Philando Castile (minor traffic stop)
- Ahmaud Arbery (out jogging)

• Breonna Taylor (home sleeping)

One of the most astonishing, unforgettable, and deliberate murders by police officers happened while the victim was in handcuffs. It was alleged that the victim attempted to use a counterfeit twenty-dollar bill as the murderer used deadly force.

On May 25, 2020, Minneapolis Police officers murdered George Floyd, a 46-year-old black man. The incident was captured on video showing Derek Chauvin, the senior officer kneeling nonchalantly on George Floyd's neck as he callously extinguished life from Floyd's body for nine minutes and twenty-nine seconds.

As the world watched what happened to Floyd, people around the world became indignant and began to protest the lack of dignity shown him. People became exasperated that *a man could call upon an officer for his life, whose job it was to "serve and protect," would ignore his pleas* with measured inattention. Many in law enforcement condemned the way Mr. Floyd died. Chauvin killed, as it were, an innocent mockingbird—George Floyd.

People were angry and saddened as they had been many times before, but there was something different this time. There were almost as many Whites as there were Blacks protesting. Blacks, Whites, Asians, Latinos Italians, Germans, Muslims, Jews, Christians and non-Christians protested until

Demonstrators protest George Floyd's police custody death.

it registered with people around the world. All were outraged.

Keep in mind, George Floyd was restrained in hand-cuffs in the presence of four officers who failed to do justice and preserve his life. It was hard to accept then, as it is now. The global response was the closest to what I would call "systemic dignity." People around the world knew that the death of George Floyd was not right. The world became the collective dignity for another.

Martin Luther King, Jr., writes, "We are caught in an inescapable network of mutuality, tied in a single garment of destiny. Whatever affects one directly, affects all indirectly." Dr. Martin Luther King, Jr. —"Letter from Birmingham Jail," April 16, 1963.

CHAPTER 8

THE RATIONALE FOR DIGNITY

Rather than give the leaders in America titles of nobility such as kings and queens, the framers of the Constitution regarded that "all people" of America had dignity. Dignity later became the center of discussion and debate. Meyer and Parent (1992) states,

> the constitutional ban on titles of nobility (Article I, section 9, clause 8; section 10, clause I) was both a hedge against corruption and a gesture toward a recognition of a dignity for human beings not based on social hierarchy. (p. 6)

African slaves were excluded in the notion that "all people" or "all men were created equal." Curry, Riley, and Battistoni (2003) speak of how those of African ancestry were not considered in the Declaration of Independence.

> Even in the seven northern states that formerly abolished slavery after the Revolution, laws discriminated against people of African ancestry, restricting suffrage and travel and segregating local

schools. There is no denying the unequal treatment accorded to African slaves during the founding period. Under the law, slaves were treated not as persons, but as property. They could be bought and sold, compelled to work for their owner, and even physically abused. Laws prohibited slaves from being taught to read or write. Moreover, the institution was hereditary; a slave's children also belonged absolutely to her or his master. (p. 244)

African Americans, however, did benefit in later debates and protests for their civil rights and liberties, by bringing attention to the supposed inclusiveness of "all people" or at least "all men created equal" to mean them, too. African slaves knew themselves to be human beings, yet the ignorance of many slave owners and slavery sympathizers suggested otherwise.

Human dignity is bestowed upon a person; therefore, persons are valuable regardless of the city, state, or country where they reside or their status. Politically, states can declare individuals to be without human rights, but they cannot declare them to be without dignity. Rights may be taken away (that is, rights given by states), but dignity remains, although the level and awareness of that dignity may not be known, and even may be doubted in cases of ill treatment and enslavement.

The matter of dignity among many Christians is a matter of faith. On one hand, many in the Christian community believe God bestowed dignity in complete measure upon humanity at creation without distinguishing gender, class, or race as criteria. However, many in the "Christian community" had doubts when it came to African slaves.

Dignity is a matter of faith. It is through that faith that love is shown toward neighbors regardless of race, ethnicity, or status. This practicality is measured and expressed by social responsibility toward others.

Geisler (1971) stresses the point "that man is responsible for his fellowman is clearly taught in Scripture." He continues his thought by adding, "What is apparently not obvious to some Christians is that this responsibility extends to social as well as the spiritual ones" (p. 178).

Therefore, in a practical sense, when one is in poverty or treated disrespectfully without fair justice based on their race, gender, or class, their perception of worth can become distorted. When this practice is promoted among "Christians," Geisler would say this is a lack of responsibility. Practical faith says one should be concerned in such a way as to relieve suffering where possible.

Man was created in the image of God according to the Bible and therefore has the responsibility of stewardship toward His creation, which includes humanity. The Stewardship Department of the General Conference suggests "shared governance began at creation when God appointed Adam and

Eve as rulers over this world. They were to function as His representatives, managing His affairs on earth" (2006, p. 11).

Pritchard (1972) suggests the issue of "human dignity has not fared well under the contemporary moral philosophy" (p. 299). In a practical sense, however, these philosophers did see the need of addressing human dignity. Pritchard adds, "They can understand why blacks feel it is so important that their children develop black pride. They can feel indignation as a direct result of oppression, exploitation, degradation, and injustice in any of their forms" (p. 299). Yet according to Pritchard, these same moral philosophers retreated from practical involvement for human dignity.

Pritchard (1972) also proposed that there is a connection between justice and dignity, and he believes there are "morally reactive attitudes" as Strawson (as cited in Pritchard) suggests in the experiences of life. "As indignation, resentment, guilt, and shame . . . they are typical manifestations of both a sense of justice and a sense of dignity" (p. 300). Pritchard further suggests,

> Those who try to formulate substantial principles of justice should reserve a prominent place for human dignity. If this is not done, the distinctively moral aspects of justice will be absent; and the claims of justice will be at best legalistic and at worse arbitrary . . . the lower one's regard is for his own dignity, the less perceptive he will be of

injustices done to him . . . the lower one has for the dignity of another, the less perceptive he will be of injustices to that other. (pp. 300, 301)

Speaking on injustice, Bryan Stevenson is known for saying "the opposite of poverty is not wealth; the opposite of poverty is justice." Patton Dodd (2017) attempts to explain what Stevenson means:

> Poverty is not just the simple absence of wealth. Poverty is the social condition of being disfavored. Since poverty tends to be geographically concentrated, it has less to do with who you are than where you live. Impoverished communities lack access, and even the hope of access, to proper education, sound and safe homes, decent jobs, reasonable healthcare. Most neighborhoods in America today can assume such access. But people in impoverished communities do without— and that has enormous consequences for their opportunities in life.

The reality of the above statements can be verified in many impoverished communities. But what about justice, and how does it play into the difficult questions of poverty and justice? Once again Dodd attempts to explain what Stevenson means by "the opposite of poverty is justice":

> Justice is not just a fair hearing in court. Justice is the ongoing effort to ensure that all citizens have

good opportunities. It is a social commitment to equality—the very thing the Declaration of Independence suggests is the impetus of the American project. The radical claim that all of us are created equal and have the right to pursue a good and full life is our country's north star. Justice is the most important measurement of how well we are doing as a country. Justice is the opposite of poverty because widespread poverty can only happen in the absence of justice.

Morris (1946) calls the belief of inherent dignity for human beings an "atomistic way" of looking at man's dignity. The atomistic way would say no more for humans than a rock would say for humans. It has atoms. Does it also have dignity? Dignity embraces more than the "atomistic way."

Morris believes human beings do exist with distinctions from all other beings, but he cautions against those who see humanity's dignity as simply one's body. He believes one must consider human values. In order for human beings to do this, Morris (1946) believes there must be a consciousness of who they are. He does not pause here but believes with John Locke, an English empiricist philosopher (1632–1704), that humanity must also have those "continuities which makes life human" (p. 58). For Morris the function of memory would be one of those continuities of human beings, in order to have an experienced life.

Dales (1977) contends that in the medieval age it was standard belief that dignity or worth came from the knowledge that humanity was created by God, in His image, and that humanity possesses the capability to have dominance over all other creatures, therefore having dignity (p. 557).

Dales continues with the work of Robert Bultot, who has, as Dales says, done more special studies on dignity than anyone. Dales says Bultot reveals there was a weakness in the medieval thought on dignity:

> He asserts that dominated Augustinian concepts of dualism of body and soul, they lack firm conception of human unity and considered the image and likeness of God to exist in the soul only. It was not, he says, until St. Thomas, with the help of Aristotle, devised a clear concept of human unity that this defect in Latin thought on human dignity was remedied. (p. 558)

This remedy meant that the person as a whole has dignity. It should not be divided between soul and body. Other studies focused on what humanity is and not just what humanity was able to *do*.

Schachter (1983) gives a rationale for having a definition for human dignity when he makes a valid point on why there is a need to come to a clear definition for dignity. His point is without a clear idea of meaning it may be impossible to "reject a specious use of the conception" (p. 849). He goes on to give the meaning of dignity by giving the etymological understanding of the root word. Schachter writes, "The Latin 'digniatas' translated as worth (in French, valeur) is a good place to begin" (p. 849).

Schachter (1983) goes on to give an analysis of the psychological implications of dignity when he states,

> Indeed, nothing is so clearly violative of the dignity of persons as treatment that demeans or humiliates them. This includes not only attacks on personal beliefs and ways of life but also attacks on the groups and communities with which individuals are affiliated . . . destroying or reducing the sense of self-respect that is so important to the integrity of every human. (p. 850)

The affront to dignity can also be seen on the economic side, which is exigent in nature. Schachter (1983) contends,

> We are led more deeply into the analysis of human dignity when we consider its relation to the material needs of human beings and to the ideal of distributive justice. Few will dispute that a person in abject condition, deprived of adequate means of subsistence, or denied the opportunity to work, suffers a profound affront to his sense of dignity and intrinsic worth. Economic and social arrangements cannot therefore be excluded from a consideration of the demands of dignity. (p. 851)

The above statement stresses the need to alleviate the conditions of those in poverty, to have their basic needs of food, housing, and employment met.

Schachter (1983) gives a listing of his conduct ideas, that are incompatible with dignity, and offends a person's worth. One example would be the humiliation of one's ancestry, "that demean and humiliate individuals or groups because of their origins, status or beliefs" (p. 852). Schachter would say this is an affront to worth.

Human dignity is important to human rights. Human rights come from the substantive understanding of human dignity. Both are devoted to how persons are to be viewed and treated.

The equality of one is equal to the equality of another. In America there are no kings and queens. However, the worth of some was not acknowledged, as they should have been, some were alienated from dignity and the rights that others seem to possess.

Consequently, a hierarchy of class is incongruent to the establishment of equality when those at the top are out of touch with those at the bottom.

CHAPTER 9

DIGNITY AND AFRICAN ANCESTRY

Berger (2008), the founder of the Roland Berger Foundation for Human Dignity, is quoted as saying, "Human dignity and human rights are precious goods that must be defended," explaining why he has established the Human Dignity Award. Berger further states, "This issue will remain important as long as human dignity is being violated thousands of times each day around the world." Berger speaks forcefully against the modern trafficking of slaves, which has changed the lives of human beings forever.

Although the enslavement of Africans in America ended on paper in the mid-1860s, the implications of unstable human relationships, human dignity, and human rights continue to exist today. This can be seen by how their descendants live lives of stress as a result of inadequacies, lack of opportunities, and ungodly treatment.

The definition of human dignity is debated in literature, in practice and theory. There are scholars like Howard and

Donnelly who say people often "confuse human rights with human dignity" (1986, p. 801); others see the need to separate the two. Indeed, Howard and Donnelly believe "human rights and human dignity are quite distinct notions" (p. 801). *Human dignity is seen as the character that is uniquely who a person is, a person of worth and value.* This definition is expanded and confirmed in its meaning by Gewirth (as cited in a dissertation abstract by Shipungin, 2003) who writes, "Human dignity is defined as the inherent human worth of all people, regardless of their specific characteristics, behaviors, or feelings about themselves" (p. 5).

Human rights according to Howard and Donnelly (1986) are the "equal and inalienable rights, in the strong sense of entitlements" (p. 802). In other words, an individual is recognized as a human and therefore entitled to human rights by a political regime.

Howard and Donnelly (1986) call human rights a "social practice that aims to realize a distinctive substantive conception of human dignity" (p. 802). It appears that they recognize the worth of individuals as human beings, having rights, thereby treated equally and fairly because they are human beings. Especially would this be true if the political entity is based on fair and equal justice for all.

Though the treatment of citizens and non-citizens may

vary in many political and governmental bodies, human dignity imposes human rights on these governments when others verify human dignity in that society.

Garbooshian (2006) suggests "there is something special in man, whether this be reason, or man's moral liberty, which allows him to choose right conduct or vicious conduct" (p. 2). Garbooshian further states:

> Authors, going back to Antiquity have often contrasted these human attributes to those of the animal or brute kingdom. That is, authors, in encouraging man to use reason, referring to judgment and the comparison of ideas so as to act in a just manner, would distinguish him from the brutes." (pp. 2, 3)

Other definitions that span many years are cited in Garbooshian's dissertation on human dignity in the eighteenth century. These definitions or strands of dignity are important because many existed during the enslavement of Africans in the United States.

These definitions or strands were indicators and instructors of dignity, conveying how humans were to be treated at that time.

The twelve (12) definitions below, cited by Garbooshian (2006) bolster the fact that dignity for *African Americans was trivial, ignored, and became a constant struggle in*

123

many ways. [Emphasis in the form of underlining and italics supplied.]

> 1. It is stated in the *Oxford Companion to Philosophy* that Plato, among others, claimed that *men could be distinguished from other beings in their rational ability . . . to the use of reason and contemplation . . .* Reason is what can know the eternal . . . not subject to the imperfections of the body" (p. 3).

> 2. The *West Minster Dictionary of Christian Ethics* also defines human dignity as "the inherent worth or value of a person" (p. 3).

> 3. In addressing human dignity Pico della Mirandola, the author of Oration, is viewed by William Craven and many other scholars as asserting *"mankind has the free will to choose what he will become."* It further states that Craven believes, "according to Cassirer's reading of Mirandola, *man's dignity is found in his ability to transform himself into the likeness of any being, and this creative power is God-like"* (pp. 3, 4).

> 4. Another said, "Mirandola also believes that man achieves dignity *through philosophy or contemplation of the divine through theology"* (p. 4).

> 5. Garbooshian suggests, "Dignity in the eighteenth century referred basically to *inherent worth or to man's reflection of God through acts, through virtue, or charity and kind and useful acts towards others"* (p. 4).

6. "Man's ability to reason and to know God through reason" was also a consideration for some (p. 4).

7. *"Man's ability to gain salvation"* was seen by some, especially by Christians in that other beings did not appear to have the same ability (p. 5).

8. Many believed during the Enlightenment that humankind's dignity was *"in his efforts, in his faculties and capacities as natural being"* (p. 5).

9. Another Enlightenment definition suggested human dignity was *"the consequence of man being created in the image of God"* (p. 5).

10. Paul Oskar Kristellera, a scholar on renaissance humanism, "states that [Pico and Ficino] justify man's dignity in terms of his metaphysical position. For Ficino [a humanist of the middle to late 1400s] *man's dignity is based on his ability to imitate or reach God."* On the other hand, Pico "dispenses with the concept of the Chain of Being by placing man outside the creation . . . with the ability to contemplate His creation" and to make choices with freedom concerning what he wants to become. *"His dignity is found in the choice of the highest form in life, both moral and intellectual."* It is asserted *"that for Pico, dignity is not "something that is given to [humankind] with his birth . . . but rather something he has to attain . . . through his own effort"* (p. 6).

11. Though "animals possess a likeness to man in their ability to feel and to be loyal, they are also considered solely dependent upon bodily functions and sensations." *Humankind on the other hand is progressive,*

"defined as the ability to compare ideas and to form clear ideas and judgments . . . and his ability to form moral judgments, or to know right from wrong, and what is more to know the existence of God" (pp. 7, 8).

12. "In the Encyclopedie, from one signifying rank, to a meaning indicating inherent worth . . . the article "Esclavage," . . . denounces slavery on moral grounds. There slavery . . . violates man's natural, inherent right to liberty, which is the basis of his dignity" (pp. 9, 10).

There is nothing in these attainments of dignity that would preclude dignity of African ancestry, although some erroneously thought there were. Here is a list describing in detail slaves' capability to have dignity as much as any other human created by God.

1. Slaves were human and therefore distinguished from animals.
   Slaves knew themselves to be human but were treated as animals.
2. Slaves had worth and value.
   Slaves were sold but knew they had human dignity (worth).
3. Slaves had challenges in exercising their freewill due to their bondage.
   Some slaves chose freewill to escape, die, or be killed rather than be a slave.

126

4. Slaves could contemplate divine (heavenly) things.

 Slaves would sing, "I am bound for Canaan land"

5. Slaves were a reflection of their Creator doing kind acts.

 Slaves helped other slaves escape to freedom and sympathized with others.

6. Slaves could know God.

 Slaves could know God when allowed to read the Bible.

7. Slaves could gain salvation.

 Slaves accepted salvation but what they wanted most was to be free.

8. Slaves had capacities and abilities as human beings.

 Slave owners depended on these capacities and abilities daily.

9. Slaves were created in the image of God.

 Slaves had the capacity to be in relationships with God and others.

10. Slaves could grasp God as intellectual and moral beings.

 Slaves knew right and wrong treatment and desired to be educated.

11. Slaves could compare ideas and form moral judgments.

 Slaves planned on their freedom; its time, when, how and where to.

12. Slaves had the right to liberty.

    Slaves were not different from other people desiring to be free.

African slaves clearly met the criteria of having dignity. Though all realizations do not receive the same significance, they do provide the thinking on dignity from antiquity to the Renaissance and on to the Enlightenment and beyond.

    Rosen (2012) says Immanuel Kant's understanding of dignity imparted something significant. Kant says only human beings have morality. Kant's morality however did not come from God; it came from within rational autonomous human beings.

> Kant's conception makes an exception of human beings from the rest of creation. Only morality has dignity and only human beings carry the moral law within themselves, so it would be wrong to think of human beings as part of the natural world in the way that rivers, trees, or dogs are. Yet Kant's conception of dignity is at the same time deeply egalitarian. Dignity is something that all human beings have in common. (p. 24)

During the Enlightenment period the idea of human dignity took on a noteworthy meaning. Dignity for some meant that a person was a part of a ranking social order. Meyer and Parent

(1992) with an interest in human dignity, describe the debate of dignity in France as follows:

> On the one hand, some political thinkers used the idea of dignity to refer to a recognized and established social hierarchy—for example, the dignity of a king, of a noble, or of a bishop. For these thinkers a person's dignity was simply a function, or a sign, of an individual's elevated social rank. In contradistinction other thinkers understood the notion of dignity to have a much wider application—for example, the dignity of man or the dignity of humanity. (p. 4)

With the social hierarchy example, only social functioning elites could have dignity. This view is very different from being possessors of dignity for simply being human. These debates of contradictions concerning dignity no doubt occurred in other localities but seemed to be exchanged in France and America in critical ways that excluded titles such as kings and queens.

The issues of indignity among African Americans are noticeable through various ideas of dignity. The first idea of dignity is the idea of "rank" among individuals. This is seen as a hierarchal-type elevation or rise to status, socially over others in a wider context (kings, queens, lords/vassals, masters/slaves, rich/poor, educated/uneducated, etc.). Those of "elevated rank" in society at the top are deemed to be possessors of dignity.

Therefore, since African ancestries were deemed to start at the bottom as enslaved, with an existence lacking dignity, being denied rank, they are left basically without options. Without political powers, limited movement to advance and improve opportunities, favoring therefore a pathway leading to poverty that makes the prospect of elevation by rank marginal.

A study *Wealth and Culture in the South* US History (n.d.) reveals,

> Wealthy plantation owners . . . came close to forming an American ruling class in the years before the Civil War. They helped shape foreign and domestic policy with one goal in view: to expand the power and reach of the cotton kingdom of the South. Socially, they cultivated a refined manner and believed whites, especially members of their class, should not perform manual labor. Rather, they created an identity for themselves based on a world of leisure in which horse racing and entertainment mattered greatly, and where the enslavement of others was the bedrock of civilization. Below the wealthy planters were the yeoman farmers, or small landowners. Below yeomen were poor, landless whites, who made up the majority of whites in the South. These landless white men dreamed of owning land and slaves and served as slave overseers, drivers, and traders in the southern economy. In fact, owning land and slaves provided one of the only opportunities for upward social and economic mobility. In the South, living the American dream meant possessing slaves, producing cotton, and owning land.

This idea of wealth and culture are reflected today in the rates of unemployment and employment opportunities when people are looked over because of race or other prejudicial factors. *Diversity can be an enlightening experience and can make a better learning, working and living environment.*

The *second idea* of dignity advances the idea of equality among humankind. George Kateb in his book *Dignity* writes, "All individuals are equal; no other species is equal to humanity" (p. 6). In Europe first, and in the establishment of the United States, the idea of equality was lacking.

With the Declaration of Independence in America, the idea of "all men created equal by their Creator" was lacking. Some of the framers of the Declaration of Independence owned slaves. This meant there was an unequal relationship between them.

For the slave, this second idea of equality was trivial. *It led to the belief that many slaves could be treated as inferior beings.* As late as 1968, Martin Luther King Jr. tried to get America to understand that African Americans were not treated as equals. Dr. King said in his famous speech, "I've been to the mountaintop," on April 3, 1968. "All we say to America is, '*Be true to what you said on paper'*

In Memphis, Tennessee, there was an injunction placed on African Americans when they protested. King's point was

Martin Luther King Jr. at a press conference in Cambridge, Mass., April 23, 1967.

that basic human rights should be applied to African Americans as they protested, according to the First Amendment of the Constitution, which states,

> Congress shall make no law respecting an establishment of religion, or prohibiting the free exercise thereof; or abridging the freedom of speech, or of the press; or the right of the people peaceably to assemble, and to petition the Government for a redress of grievances.

Martin L. King, Jr.'s (1968) response was brilliant. As a citizen of the country, he responded:

> If I lived in China or even Russia, or any totalitarian country, maybe I could understand the denial of certain basic First Amendment privileges, because they hadn't committed themselves to that

over there. But somewhere I read of the freedom of assembly. Somewhere I read of the freedom of speech. Somewhere I read of the freedom of the press. Somewhere I read that the greatness of America is the right to protest for right. And so just as I say, we aren't going to let any injunction turn us around.

Introduced previously, inequality and the lack of dignity can lead to poverty, and poverty leads to a number of issues. These include the lack of education, the lack of proper legal representation, the lack of medical health, and greater than ought, incarceration rates. All of these are complications of great concern in the African American community.

In an interview with Oprah Winfrey, Bryan Stevenson (2015) of the Innocence Project says, "We have a system of justice that treats you better if you're rich and guilty than if you're poor and innocent. Wealth–not culpability–shapes outcomes."

The *third idea* of dignity deals with the distinction of humankind from all other creations such as animals, plants, or objects. Humankind is unique with superior qualities of intellect. No other species has the ability to be a steward for planet earth and the animal kingdom.

In a peculiar way, there have been discussions on whether embedded in African Americans are innate pathologies, which cause them to be welfare recipients suited for poverty, prone towards criminality, and deviant behaviors. According to Larry Adelman (n.d.) creator and producer of "Race: the Power of Illusion":

> Ethnic cleansing, affirmative action battles, immigration restrictions—all place race at center stage in contemporary life. Race is so fundamental to discussions of poverty, education, crime, music, and sports that, whether we are racist or anti-racist, we rarely question its reality. . . . One hundred years ago many whites felt that high African American disease and mortality rates were caused not by poverty, poor sanitation, and Jim Crow but because black people were inherently infirm and destined to die out. When influential Prudential Insurance Company statistician Frederick Hoffman compared death and disease rates between white and black people in 1896, he attributed the disparities to a "heritable race trait" among Negroes, ignoring the impact of poverty, poor sanitation, and over-crowding on health and mortality. Today, it is still popular to attribute group differences in performance to innate "racial" traits.

Human beings have the superior ability to contemplate and study; the ability to make choices and judgments. Furthermore, humankind's ability to build cars, airplanes, and computers places them in a category of their own.

It is well documented that African slaves were erroneously regarded as nonhuman, beastly in nature, expected not just to work, but work as beastly animals do.

Michael E. Ruane (2019) reporter for the Washington Post details how scientific racism was a deceptive practice:

> A decade before the Civil War was part of the long, insidious practice of what historians call scientific racism — the spread of bogus theories of supposed black inferiority in an attempt to rationalize slavery and centuries of social and economic domination and plunder. Here, enslaved people were beneath even the human desire for freedom. They had to be diseased. This thinking would thrive in the 18th and especially the 19th centuries. It would mutate, vary in perversion and persevere for 400 years right up to the present day. Starting with theories of physical and intellectual inferiority that likened blacks to animals — monkeys and apes especially — or helpless children, it would evolve to infer black cultural and then social inferiority.

Slaves were human beings, but they were not compensated for their labor; they were treated as animals. According to one professor, and others agree, *an estimated amount for unpaid labor would be in the trillions of dollars.* Hadivi, T. (2020) contends, "William Darity, professor of public policy at Duke University, estimates a concrete program could cost the U.S. government between $10 trillion and $12 trillion." Their decendants were seen as incapable of intellect, needing to be coerced, trained and regulated to belittling low-paying jobs, which supported indignity and led to poverty.

Michael E. Ruane (2019) continues with this thought,

> Such thought exists today with pernicious assumptions about the current nature of black life and black people, still featuring age-old racist references to blacks as animals. It persists despite the advent of modern DNA science, which has shown race to be fundamentally a social construct. Humans, as it turns out, share about 99.9 percent of their DNA with each other, and outward physical characteristics such as hair texture and skin color, about which racists have long obsessed, occupy just a tiny portion of the human genome.

With the many intellectual inventions by African Americans and their educational endeavors, astronauts were able to explore space as seen in the true story "Hidden Figures" written by Margot Lee Shetterly (2016) who says,

> Before John Glenn orbited the earth, or Neil Armstrong walked on the moon, a group of dedicated female mathematicians known as "human computers" used pencils, slide rules, and adding machines to calculate the numbers that would launch rockets, and astronauts, into space . . . Dorothy Vaughan, Mary Jackson, Katherine Johnson, and Christine Darden, lived through the Civil Rights era, the Space Race, the Cold War, and the move-

ment for gender equality, and whose work forever changed the face of NASA and the country.

The *fourth idea* of dignity is the idea of how one should be
treated with respect. The historical mistreatment and disrespect
of enslaved Africans and their descendants is already detailed in
the third and fourth chapters of this book.

The *fifth idea* of dignity revolves around attitude, position or deportment. African Americans were expected to maintain docile attitudes. When dignity is omitted, injustice is left to
continue, as it violates the conscious. A person who stands in a
dignified manner against injustice, resisting despite difficulties,
is a person of dignity. Such was the case with Fredrick Doug-
lass, Harriet Tubman, Martin Luther King, Rosa Parks, White
abolitionists like William Lloyd Garrison, Harriet Beecher
Stowe, John Brown, and Angelina Grimke and others.

Martin Luther King's method was based on a position of
using non-violent protest, and it was effective in bringing about
change. It was an unassuming resistance through strength and love.

An early understanding of the word dignity only applied
to those who were the elevated ones. This meant then, that there
was no equality except for the "dignified elevated ones". If we
are to survive, all humanity must be recognized as having been
created equally and thus should be treated equally.

CHAPTER 10

BESTOWAL OF DIGNITY

In Garbooshian's work it was communicated that one of the ways to attain dignity, considered by some, was the ability to gain salvation and to know God. However, works and efforts of humanity are needed to gain this "brand of dignity" because the focus is on what you do to gain salvation, and what you *do* to gain dignity for that matter.

There is dignity that comes from God and it is entirely different. The key point about God's dignity is that humans' ability to gain it through choice is not the basis for dignity. Instead, *dignity that comes from God is bestowed equally upon all humanity, and is therefore not attained by anything we do or the decisions we make.*
What if there was something that a person could do to attain dignity but he/she failed to attain it, or what if the choices that are made are not perfect, but less than perfect? What then?

Genesis 2:7 states, "And the Lord God formed man of the dust of the ground, and breathed into his nostrils the

138

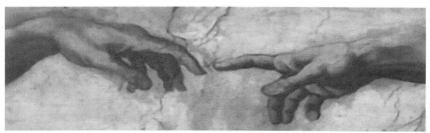

The Creation of Adam by Michelangelo forms part of the painting on the ceiling of the Sistine Chapel in Vatican City.

breath of life; and man became a living soul." Genesis 1:26 and 27 says, "Then God said, 'Let us make mankind in our image, in our likeness.'" The phrase "the image of God" has had vigorous arguments over its meaning according to Pollard (2011),

> The word translated "image" (Hebrew, tselem) is used to convey the idea of the "shadow" or "reflection" of God." While theologians have argued about what constitutes "the image of God," textual clues in Genesis 1-3 suggest that (1) the "image of God" is that quality of human existence that differentiates it from the rest of creational life, since the phrase is only applied to the creation of human beings; (2) those features of humanity that give humans their unique similarity to and relationship with God; (3) those particular endowments, such as conceptive and discursive rationality (Genesis 2:19, 20); individual and communal relationality (Genesis 2: 23, 24; 5:20); moral and ethical agency (Genesis 3:14); vocational responsibility (Genesis 2:15); and aesthetic sensitivity (Genesis 2:19).

139

What is prominent are the words, "Let (Us)" in "(Our)" image. Who are those who are known as "(Us and Our)"? The answer to this question has implications as to the origin of dignity.

Bible scholars believe that "Us and Our" speak of (Father, Son, Holy Spirit) the Godhead. That means these three— God the Father, God the Son, and God the Holy Spirit—jointly rule heaven and earth as sovereign creators, superior and elevated above angels, humans and everything else in creation.

Remember the hierarchy of Western Europe? Its notion of dignity for slaves was just that—a notion.

EUROPEAN DIGNITY PYRAMID

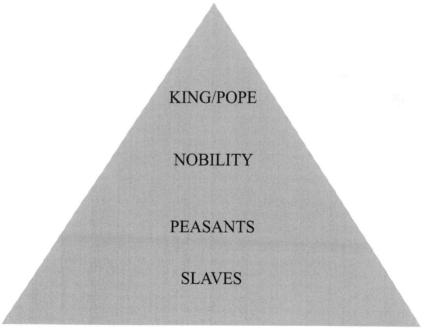

KING/POPE

NOBILITY

PEASANTS

SLAVES

Figure 10.1

The Godhead works in a completely harmonious way. An example: their self-sacrificing love is how humans are to work with each other.

The hierarchal order of the Godhead is not a hierarchy. It is known as the Trinity. Calvin B. Rock writes,

> The Trinity is not aligned in a hierarchy of authority or importance. Of course, this notion is foreign to us humans. For us there is always a first and last, a lesser and better, a major and a minor- but not so with the Godhead. They relate as three equal lines in a circle, and they are indistinguishable in motive, inseparable in purpose, and indivisible in power (p. 90).

It is a co-equal oneness of love and agreement of three all-powerful beings, with the ability to create mankind and bestow dignity upon all humanity equally.

Instead of placing some in humanity ahead of others, as unequal beings; humanity was made in such a way that included humanity in the image and likeness of the Godhead.

GODHEAD

Father, Son, Holy Spirit
Encircles Humanity

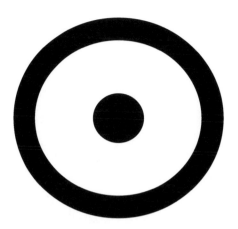

1. This model of the Godhead encircling humanity is perfect for demonstrating what dignity is about.

2. It is about <u>relationship</u>—an association with God. The dot in the circle represents humanity created by God and encircled by God.

3. The complement to relationship is <u>oneness,</u> a unity *with* the Maker.

4. The Godhead <u>supplies everything</u> needed in this relationship for it to exist. They supply all the basic things like water, food, and air. Everything that exists came through their creative works. Humanity can be comforted in knowing "God is our refuge and strength, a very present help in trouble" Psalm 46:1.

5. God made humanity equal: no one individual has more worth than another.

6. God made humanity different from animals with many abilities: humans are not beasts and certainly not the least of creation.

7. God elevated humanity by making them in their image.

8. Humanity was made with honor and morality.

9. Humanity was made with status, rank, equality, position, and respect and was given dominion over the rest of creation.

The *relationship factor* is so important to dignity that when humanity faltered (sin), the love of God was so strong that God made the move to restore, to let it be known, that all is not lost.

1. God sought humanity after they faltered.

2. God was *with* Joseph when he was sold as a slave, then Joseph became the second in command to Pharaoh.

3. God was *with* Moses when sent to tell Pharaoh "Let my people go."

4. God was *with* His People when He led them through the Red Sea.

5. God was *with* David when he slew the giant Goliath.

6. God showed up in the burning fiery furnace *with* Shadrach, Meshach, and Abednego.

7. God was *with* Daniel and shut the mouths of the lions.

8. God came to be *with* humanity by being God in the flesh as Jesus, who lived and died to restore us. (John 1:1–3, 14) Three major religious beliefs (Muslims, Jews, and Christianity) support the idea that Jesus was a historical living person.

9. God came down from heaven, was born in Bethlehem and is called Immanuel, meaning "God with us."

GODHEAD
Father, Holy Spirit

This model of the Godhead features the Son, now in a dual role as Son of God and Son of Man, God with us.

10. God provided forgiveness, which is what humanity should ask for when they sin.

11. God provided an answer to the sin problem by putting Himself on the line and by paying the cost through the death of His Son.

12. Once again humanity is elevated—first by creation and second by redemption. The Son according to the Bible provided redemption and sets humanity free to be a slave no longer. (John 8: 36) "If the Son therefore shall make you free, you shall be free indeed."

The Godhead (US/OUR) created everything that exists, and humanity was the apple of their eye. The Bible says, Psalm 17:8: "Keep me as the apple of the eye, hide me under the shadow of thy wings." Zechariah 2:8, "For thus saith the LORD of hosts; After the glory hath he sent me unto the nations which spoiled you: for he that toucheth you toucheth the apple of his eye."

In the African American experience, the belief in God gave hope and the understanding of dignity. There is a bestowal of dignity from the Godhead and African Americans are undeniably included and created in God's image. God's covenant with Abraham in Genesis 12:3, "in thee shall all families of the earth be blessed." In revelation 7:9 all nations are represented around the throne of God. This truth has been suppressed in a number of ways.

Like the sun, moon and stars, the dignity that comes from God is unalterable and untouchable by mankind. Others may diminish the awareness of that dignity, but it cannot be taken away. Is it possible for a descendant from an African

Image credit: obamawhitehouse.archives.gov
Barack Obama,
44th President of the United States

country to become the President of the United States?
President Obama says, "Yes, we can!"

African slaves found worship services and sermons
filled with the thought that there would be a better day and that
the God of all the earth will judge wrongdoing in a just way.

About 188 years after slaves were sold for economic
development in the nation's capital, Brown (2018) writes:

> In 2016, Georgetown University in Washington,
> D.C., offered a public apology after acknowledg-
> ing that 188 years prior, Jesuit priests sold 272

slaves to save the school from financial ruin. This is how The New York Times first reported the story: The human cargo was loaded on ships at a bustling wharf in the nation's capital, destined for the plantations of the Deep South. Some slaves pleaded for rosaries as they were rounded up, praying for deliverance. But on that day, in the fall of 1838, no one was spared: not the 2-month-old baby and her mother, not the field hands, not the shoemaker, and not Cornelius Hawkins, who was about 13 years old when he was forced onboard. Their panic and desperation would be mostly forgotten for more than a century. But this was no ordinary slave sale. The enslaved African-Americans had belonged to the nation's most prominent Jesuit priests. And they were sold, along with scores of others, to help secure the future of the premier Catholic institution of higher learning at the time, known today as Georgetown University.

Nicholas Miller (2017) believes there is a similarity between Martin Luther King, Jr. and Martin Luther when he writes, "an interesting parallel with Luther's efforts in 1517 and the following years. We most often think about Martin Luther in connection with justification by faith, the authority of Scripture, and the centrality of grace."

Miller later connects the parallel of the two Martin Luther's in a way that shows how the notion of economic materialism might interfere with human dignity.

> MLK accused the American government of allowing materialism and avarice to interfere with and "poison" the American soul in its relation to universal love for humanity; so Luther criticizes the power structure of his day for allowing the materialism of the system of indulgences to blind church members to the true pathway to God of repentance and grace.

In the end, King believed that the idea of dignity was based on being made in the image of God. Outlined below are the four components that he believed would enable humanity to live in a "beloved community":

> The foundations of MLK's thought regarding human dignity lie in the universal truth of the image of God in humanity. As one MLK scholar summarized it, King built this idea of human dignity on four related points: 1. All persons are children of God and have equal value and dignity. 2. This equal worth becomes the basis of "just and fair treatment." 3. This dignity brings with it a moral capacity that gives people the ability to make socially good choices. 4. This shared image of God provides the "existential common ground" for genuine community building across races, cultures, and ethnicities, making the "beloved community . . . a distinct historical possibility."

To believe in God and a concern for others is consistent with the dignity of humanity. For this is what the Godhead said and did:

> The Spirit of the Lord is upon me, because he hath anointed me to preach the gospel to the poor; he hath sent me to heal the brokenhearted, to preach deliverance to the captives, and recovering of sight to the blind, to set at liberty them that are bruised (Luke 4:18).

> Learn to do good; seek justice, correct oppression; bring justice to the fatherless, plead the widow's cause (Isaiah 1:17).

> He has told you, O man, what is good; and what does the Lord require of you but to do justice, and to love kindness, and to walk humbly with your God? (Micah 6:8)

Abraham Lincoln's Gettysburg Address expresses how terminal the lack of dignity can be, if priest, kings and politicians ignore it as reflected below.

> Four score and seven years ago our fathers brought forth on this continent a new nation, conceived in Liberty, and dedicated to the proposition that all men are created equal. "Now we are engaged in a great civil war, testing whether that nation or any nation so conceived and so dedicated, can long endure. We are met on a great battlefield of that war. We have come to dedicate a portion of that field, as a final resting place for those who here gave their lives that that nation

might live. It is altogether fitting and proper that we should do this. "But, in a larger sense, we can not dedicate—we can not consecrate—we can not hallow—this ground. The brave men, living and dead, who struggled here, have consecrated it, far above our poor power to add or detract. The world will little note, nor long remember what we say here, but it can never forget what they did here. It is for us the living, rather, to be dedicated here to the unfinished work which they who fought here have thus far so nobly advanced. It is rather for us to be here dedicated to the great task remaining before us—that from these honored dead we take increased devotion to that cause for which they gave the last full measure of devotion—that we here highly resolve that these dead shall not have died in vain—that this nation, under God, shall have a new birth of freedom—and that government of the people, by the people, for the people, shall not perish from the earth.

Raines (2019) a reporter, writes on finding the last ship to carry slaves to America says, "Out of 20,000 ships used in the global slave trade, just 13 have been found" but the last one believed to come to America was found - The Clotilda. It arrived at Mobile Bay, Alabama around 1860. The descendants of those slaves still live in that area which is known now as Africa Town.

One day the secrets of the dead will be revealed, even kings will have to bring their man-made glory to the King of Kings and bow as the wise men of the east did centuries ago. Earthly powers, earthly towers, and earthly crowns will all come down. The challenge for dignity and its beneficiary human rights must continue and we must remain hopeful and confident until:

> The kingdoms of this world are become the kingdoms of our Lord, and of his Christ; and he shall reign for ever and ever (Revelation 11:15)

This will be the glory of the redeemed. Psalm 63 (NIV) says,

> Because your love is better than life,
> my lips will glorify you . . .
> with singing lips my mouth will praise you.

How can I keep from singing?

REFERENCE LIST

Abraham Lincoln Online (n.d.). House Divided Speech by Abraham Lincoln. Retrieved from http://showcase.netins.net/ web/creative/lincoln/speeches/ house.htm

Abouzeid, R. (2011, January 21). Bouazizi: The man who set himself and Tunisia on fire. Time Magazine [Electronic version]. Retrieved from http://www.time.com/time/ world/ article/0,8599,2043557,00.html

Adi, H. (2012). Africa and the Transatlantic SlaveTrade. http://www. bbc.co.uk/history/british/abolition/africa_article_01.shtml

Alderman, L. (n.d.). Race the power of illusion. Retrieved from http://newsreel.org/guides/race/pressreleasecredit.htm

African Americans: The state of the disparity. Retrieved from http://www .caa.wa.gov/priorities/civil/documents/StateoftheDisparity12306 version32.pdf

Allison, L. (2009, October 17). Link made between poverty and learning. Suite 101.com, Retrieved from http://www. suite101.com/content/link-made-between-poverty-and-learning-a159772

American government: Obstacles to voting. (n.d.). Retrieved from http://www.cliffsnotes.com/WileyCDA/CliffsReviewTopic/Obstacles-to-Voting.topicArticleId-65383,articleId-65525.html

Anderson, S. (2011 Oct. 24). The great days of sail, slavery, ships, and sickness https://www.gresham.ac.uk/lecture/transcript/print/slavery-ships-and-sickness/

Andrews, E. (2019). How many U.S. presidents owned enslaved people. https://www.history.com/news/how-many-u-s-presidents-owned-slaves

Baker-Fletcher, G. (1993). Somebodyness. Minneapolis, MN: Fortress Press.

Battles, M. (2013). The trans-atlantic slave trade http://ldhi.library.cofc.edu/exhibits/show/africanpassageslowcountryadapt/introductionatlanticworld/trans_atlantic_slave_trade

Benns, W. (2015). American slavery reinvented. https://www.theatlantic.com/business/archive/2015/09/prison-labor-in-america/406177/

Berger, R. (2008, November). Roland Berger foundation documents human trafficking and slavery-human dignity award goes to Somaly Nan from Cambodia. Roland Berger strategy consultants press archive. Retrieved from http://www.rolandberger.com/company/press/releases/518-press_archive2008_sc_content/ Human_Dignity_Award_2008.html

Bergner, R. (2005, June 29). Church leaders call for action on poverty. Loudon Forum on G-8. Retrieved from http://jmm.aaa.net.au/articles/15429 .htm

Blue, M. (2008, January 22). Black and white family net worth disparity true. Politifact.com. Retrieved from http://politifact.com/truth-o-meter/statements/2008/jan/22/john-edwards/

black-and-white-family-net-worth-disparity-true/

Boles, J. B. (Ed.). (1988). Masters and slaves in the house of the Lord: Race and religion in the American south 1740-1870. Lexington, KY: University Press of Kentucky.

Bromley, A. (2010, August 14). The link between poverty and obesity in America. Socyberty.com. Retrieved March from http://socyberty.com/issues/the-link-between-poverty-and-obesity-in-america/

Brown v. Board of Education. (n.d.) Retrieved from http://brown-vboard.org/summary/

Brown v. Board of Education. (n.d.) National Park Service. Retrieved from http://www.nps.gov/brvb/historyculture/kansas.htm

Brown, S. M. (2018). The major role the catholic church played in slavery. http://amsterdamnews.com/news/2018/sep/18/major-role-catholic-church-played-slavery/

Burns, K. (2009, October 5). Time Magazine,174(13), 8.

Calvin, J. (1960). Institutes of the Christian Religion. (ed. J. T. McNeil). Library of Christian Classics. (Ford Lewis Battles Trans.). Philadelphia, PA: Westminster Press.

Carson, H. M. (1977). The epistles of Paul to the Colossians and Philemon. Tyndale New Testament Commentaries. Grand Rapids, MI: Eerdmans.

Center for Disease Control. U.S. Public health service syphilis study at Tuskegee. Retrieved from http://www.cdc.gov/tuskegee/timeline.htm

Charters of Freedom. Transcript of the Constitution of the United States. Retrieved from http://www.archives.gov/exhibits/charters/ constitution_transcript.html

Choi, C. (2011, August 24). Big banks offering payday loans. The Birmingham News, p 4D.

Civil Rights Division. United States Department of Justice. (2008, July). Introduction to federal voting rights laws [Updated]. Retrieved from http://www.justice.gov/crt/voting/intro/intro.php

Conditions of Antebellum Slavery. (n.d). Retrieved from http://www .pbs.org/wgbh/aia/part4/4p2956.html

Constitutional Topic. (n.d.).The Constitutional Convention. Retrieved from http://www.usconstitution.net/consttop_ccon.html

Cornell University Law. (n.d.). Plessy v. Ferguson. Retrieved from http://www.law.cornell.edu/supct/html/historics/USSC_CR_0163_0537_ZS.html

Cozzens, L. (n.d.) After the Civil War: Introduction. Retrieved from http://www.watson.org/~lisa/blackhistory/post-civil-war/reconstruction.html

Crutchfield, R. D., & Pettinicchio, D. (2009, May). "Cultures of inequality": Ethnicity, immigration, social welfare, and imprisonment. The Annals of the American Academy of Political and Social Science, 623, 134-145.

Curry, J. A., Riley, R. B., & Battistoni, R. (2003). Constitutional government: The American experience (5th ed.). Dubuque, IA: Kendall Hunt.

Dales, R. C. (1977, October-December). A medieval view of human dignity. [Electronic version].Journal of the History of Ideas, 38(4), 557-572. University of Pennsylvania Press. Stable URL: http://www.jstor.org/stable/2708687

Daugherity B. J., & Bolton, C. C. (Eds.). (2008). With all deliberate speed. Fayetteville, AR: University of Arkansas Press.

Davis, M. (n.d.). Poverty: A holistic definition [Msg 82]. Message posted to http://hubpages.com/hub/Poverty-A-Holistic-Definition

De Oliveira, & T., Duraiappah, A. K. (n.d.). Realising development. Poverty times #2. The Environment Times Retrieved from http://www.grida.no/ publications/ et/ ep2/page.aspx

Diedrich, M., Gates, L. H. Jr., & Pedersen, C. (Eds.). (1999). Black imagination and the middle passage. New York, NY: Oxford University Press.

Dodd, P. (2017). The opposite of poverty is not wealth its justice. Retrieved July 31, 2020. https://www.folomedia.org/the-opposite-of-poverty-is-not-wealth-its-justice/

Donavan, R. (1987, March). Home care work: A legacy of slavery in U.S. health care. Affilia, 2(33-44). Retrieved from http:// aff.sagepub.com/content/2/3/33.abstract

Douglas, F. (1852). The hypocrisy of American slavery (1852 July 4 speech). Retrieved from http://www.historyplace.com/ speeches/douglass.htm

Elliott, C. (1850) Sinfulness of American slavery: Proved from its evil sources; its injustice; its wrongs; its contrariety to many scriptural commands. (Vol. 1). Cincinnati, OH: L.

Swormstedt & J. H. Power.

Elliott, D. (2003, June 11). Wallace in the schoolhouse door. Retrieved from http://www.npr.org/2003/06/11/1294680/wallace-in-the-schoolhouse-door

Elliott, S. (2016). How American Indians Reservations came to be. Retrieved from https://www.pbs.org/wgbh/roadshow/stories/articles/2015/5/25/how-american-indian-reservations-came-be

Equal Access to Public Accommodations. (n.d.). Virginia historical society. Retrieved from http://www.vahistorical.org/collections-and-resources/virginia-history-explorer/civil-rights-movement-virginia/equal-access

Eskew, G. (1997). But for Birmingham: The local and national movements in the civil rights struggle. Chapel Hill, NC: The University of North Carolina Press.

Fagin, J. R. (n.d.). Chapter 1: Basic concepts in the study of racial and ethnic relations. Retrieved from http://sociweb.tamu.edu/faculty/feagin/ Ch1RE.html

Federal Poverty Guidelines. (2009). Retrieved from http://aspe.hhs.gov/poverty/ 09poverty.shtml

Felder, C. H. (Ed.). (1991). Stony the road we trod. Minneapolis, MN: Fortress Press.

Ferris state university (2000). Jim crow museum https://www.ferris.edu/jimcrow/what.htm

Findlaw/Cases and Coeds. U.S. Supreme Court. Brown v. Board of Education. Retrieved from http://caselaw.lp.findlaw.com/scripts/getcase .pl?court=US&vol=347&invol=483

Finkelman, P. (2000, Winter). Garrison's constitution: The covenant with death and how it was made (Vol. 32, No. 4). Retrieved from http://www.archives.gov/ publications/prologue/2000/winter/garrisons-constitution-1.html

Foner, P. S. (Ed.). (1975). The voice of black America. Vol. 1: Major speeches by blacks in the United States. New York, NY: Capricorn Books.

Freeman, K. (Ed.). (1998). African American culture and heritage in higher education research and practice. Westport, CT: Praeger.

Friedlander, B. (1999). Poverty study. Retrieved http://www.news.cornell.edu/chronicle/99/4.8.99/poverty_study.html

Garbooshian, A. (2006). The concept of human dignity in the French and American enlightenments: Religion, virtue, liberty. (Doctoral dissertation, Wayne State University) Available from ProQuest Dissertations and Theses database. (UMI No. 3232080)

Garbooshian, A. (2006) The concept of human dignity in the French and American enlightenments: Religion, virtue, liberty. (Doctoral dissertation, Wayne State University, 2006) Abstract retrieved from http://proquest.umi.com/pqdweb?index =0&did=1225114311&SrchMode=1&sid=1&Fmt=2&VInst=PROD&VType=PQD&RQT=309&VName=PQD&TS=1258641207&clientId=1898

Gardner, J. (n.d.). PBS: Engineer of a great society. Retrieved from http://www.pbs.org/johngardner/chapters/4.html

Geisler, N. L. (1971). Ethics: Alternatives and issues. Grand Rapids, MI: Zondervan.

General Conference Stewardship Department, General Conference of Seventh-day Adventists. (2006). Strategic church finances. Silver Springs, MD: Stewardship Department of Seventh-day Adventists.

Gettysburg Address (n.d.) https://www.history.com/topics/american-civil-war/gettysburg-address

Goffman, E. (1956). Embarrassment and social organization. The American Journal of Sociology, 62(3), 264-271. Retrieved from http://www.jstor.org.ezproxy.cc .andrews.edu/stable/pdfplus/2772920.pdf?acceptTC=true

Guasco, M. (2017). The Misguided Focus on 1619 as the Beginning of Slavery in the U.S.Damages Our Understanding of American History https://www.smithsonianmag.com/history/misguided-focus-1619-beginning-slavery-us-damages-our-understanding-american-history-180964873/

Hadivi, T. (2020 August). Slavery reparations cost U.S. government 10 to 12 trillion. https://www.cnbc.com/2020/08/12/slavery-reparations-cost-us-government-10-to-12-trillion.html

Hagler-Geard, T. (2012 February 12). Black history month: Selma to Montgomery marchers. Retrieved from http://abcnews.go.com/blogs/headlines/2012/02/black-history-month-selma-to-montgomery-marches/

Haley, A. (1976). Roots: The saga of an American family. New York, NY: Gramercy Books.

Harrold, S. (2004). The rise of aggressive abolitionism. Lexington, KY: University Press of Kentucky.

Head, T. (n.d.). Civil liberties. History of the Atlantic Slave Trade

in America (1528-1807). Retrieved from http://civilliberty.
about.com/od/ raceequalopportunity/ig/History-of-Black-
Civil-Rights/The-Atlantic-Slave-Trade.htm

History of Jamestown (n.d.). https://www.historyisfun.org/james-
town-settlement/history-jamestown/

History trail of tears: Indian removal act. (n.d.) https://www.histo-
ry.com/topics/native-american-history/trail-of-tears

Howard, R., & Donnelly, J. (1986, Sept.). Human dignity, human
rights, and political regimes [Electronic version]. The
American Political Science Review, 80(3), 801-817. Stable
URL: http://www.jstor.org/stable/1960539

Karon, B. P. (1975). Black scars. New York, NY: Springer.

Kateb, G. (2011). Human dignity. Cambridge, MA: Harvard University Press.

Katznelson, I. (2005). When affirmative action was white. New
York, NY: W. W. Norton & Company.

Kelly, B., Baker, B., O'Donovan, S., Taylor, K., & Brown, D.
(n.d.). After slavery. Retrieved from http://www.afterslav-
ery.com/

Kappeler, V. E. (2014 January). https://plsonline.eku.edu/inside-
look/brief-history-slavery-and-origins-american-policing

King, M. L., Jr. (1963). Letter from a Birmingham jail. https://
mlk50.civilrightsmuseum.org/justice

King, M. L., Jr. (1968). 17 Inspiring Martin Luther King Jr. Quotes.
https://www.biography.com/news/martin-luther-king-fa-

mous-quotes

King, M. L., Jr. (1968). I have been to the mountaintop. https://
www.digitalhistory.uh.edu/disp_textbook.cfm?smtid=3&p-
sid=3623

King, M. L., Jr. (n.d.). (YouTube) Why I am opposed to the war
in Vietnam (Audio Speech). http://www.youtube.com/
watch?v=b80Bsw0UG-U

Loevy, R. D. (1990). To end all segregation. Lanham: MD. University Press of America.

Longenecker, R. N. (1992). Slavery. The encyclopedia of biblical
ethics. R. K. Harrison. (Ed.). Thomas Nelson. (1992). p. 386

Loyseau, C. (1987). Openlearn. https://www.open.edu/openlearn/
history-the-arts/early-modern-europe-introduction/con-
tent-section-6.1 Loyseau, [1610] 1987, p. 14)

Maddox, A. (2009, May 14-20). Politics of Brown v. Board of Education. The New York Amsterdam News, pp. 12, 31.

Mandinka-English Dictionary. (1995). Prepared by Peace Corps.
Retrieved from http://www.africanculture.dk/gambia/ftp/
mandinka.pdf

Mark, J. (2009). The seven wonders – Ancient History Encyclopedia https://www.ancient.eu/The_Seven_Wonders/

Martineau, J. (2008, April 23). U.S. has world's highest number
of prisoners. Retrieved from http://www.nowpublic.com/
world/u-s-has-worlds-highest-number-prisoners

Meyer, M. J., & Parent, W. A. (Eds.). (1992). The constitution of
rights. Ithaca, NY: Cornell University Press.

Miller, P. (2017). Human dignity. http://libertymagazine.org/article/ human-dignity

Morris, B. (1946, October). The dignity of man. [Electronic version]. Ethics, 57(1), 57-64. University of Chicago Press. Stable URL: http://www.jstor.org/stable/ 2379033

Morrissey, J. (2010, January 14). Pawnshops flourish in hard times, drawing scrutiny. Time Magazine. Retrieved from http://www. time.com/time/business/article/ 0,8599,1953095,00.html

Neiger, C. (2008, October 8). Why car title loans are a bad idea. CNN Living. Retrieved from http://articles.cnn.com/2008- 10-08/living/aa.car.title.loans_1_car-title-loan-interest- rates-responsible-lending-for-title-loans?_s=PM:LIVING

NPR radio diaries (2013 January 10) Segregation forever. Retrieved from http://www.npr.org/2013/01/14/169080969/segrega- tion-forever-a-fiery-pledge-forgiven-but-not-forgotten

Obama, B. (2006). The audacity of hope. New York, NY: Three Rivers Press.

Pascher, P. (2020) https://www.youtube.com/watch?v=AGUwcs9qJXY

PBS.org. (n.d.) Africans in America. Part 1: First Africans to Virginia. Retrieved from http://www.pbs.org/wgbh/aia/ part1/1p263.html

Philen, R. (2007). Oscar Lewis and the culture of poverty. Re- trieved from http://robertphilen.blogspot.com/2007/03/ oscar-lewis-and-culture-of-poverty.html

Pilgrim, D. (2000). What was Jim Crow? Retrieved from Ferris State University. http://www.ferris.edu/JIMCROW/what.htm

Plotkin, G. (2009, November 5). 90% of black children on food stamps. Retrieved from http://uspoverty.change.org/blog/view/90_of_black_children _on_food_stamps

Pollard, L. N. (2011). Loving leadership. Hagerstown, MD: Review and Herald.

Prison population exceeds two million. Retrieved from http://www.infoplease.com/ipa/A0881455.html

Pritchard, M. (1972, July). Human dignity and justice. [Electronic version]. Ethics, 82(84), 299-313. University of Chicago Press. Stable URL: http://www.jsto r.org/stable/2379854

Raboteau, A. J. (2004). Slave religion. Oxford, NY: Oxford University Press.

Raines, B. (2019). https://lagniappemobile.com/serial/sunken-trea-sure-a-reporters-remarkable-account-of-finding-the-last-slave-ship/

The Reinvestment Fund for the Pennsylvania Dept. of Banking. (2004, November 12). Understanding the low African American home ownership rate in southwestern Pennsylvania. Retrieved from http://www.trfund.com/resource/downloads/policypubs/TRF-Housing-Opp-Heinz.pdf

Roberts, J. D. (1974). A black political theology. Philadelphia, PA: Westminster Press.

Rock, C. B., (2014). Something better: God's gracious provisions for our daily decisions. Review and Herald Publishing Association. Hagerstown, MD.

Rosen, M. (2012). Dignity: Its history and meaning. Cambridge, MA: Harvard University Press.

Ross, T. (1990). The rhetorical tapestry of race: White innocence and black abstraction [Electronic version]. William & Mary Law Review, 32(1), article 2. http://scholarship.law.wm.edu/cgi/viewcontent.cgi?article=1917&context=wmlr&sei-redir=1#search

Ruane, M. (2019). Scientific racism: a history of the phony theory that perpetuates white supremacy. https://www.washingtonpost.com/local/a-brief-history-of-the-enduring-phony-science-that-perpetuates-white-supremacy/2019/04/29/20e-6aef0-5aeb-11e9-a00e-050dc7b82693_story.html

Sandweiss M. A. (2010, August 18). NPR American lives: The Strange tale of Clarence King. Retrieved April, 3 2021. https://www.npr.org/templates/story/story.php?storyId=129250977

Schachter, O. (1983, October). Human dignity as a normative concept [Electronic version]. The American Journal of International Law 77(4), 848-854. American Society of International Law. Stable URL: http://www.jstor.org/stable/2202536

Scott, B. (2010). A Mother's Desperate Act: 'Margaret Garner' https://www.npr.org/2010/11/17/131395936/a-mother-s-desperate-act-margaret-garner

Shetterly, M. (2016). Hidden figures. Harper Collins Publisher. New York. https://www.amazon.com/Hidden-Figures-Readers-Margot-Shetterly/dp/0062662376/ref=pd_lpo_14_t_0/136-2655829-3255266?_encod-

ing=UTF8&pd_rd_i=0062662376&pd_rd_r=3cf0bbe4-
0c36-463d-9e3a-61c18c230cf6&pd_rd_w=lg422&pd_rd_
wg=X2tNs&pf_rd_p=7b36d496-f366-4631-94d3-61b87b-
52511b&pf_rd_r=0QJ2G49F2JHFW1BQ2SF8&psc=1&re-
fRID=0QJ2G49F2JHFW1BQ2SF8#reader_0062662376

Shipungin, E. (2002). When the shoe fits: Human dignity, denial, and recognition in a shelter for homeless families. (Doctoral dissertation, Michigan State University). ProQuest PDF 179 URL: http://proquest.umi.com/pqdweb?did=765172291 &sid=1&Fmt=2&clientId=1898&RQT=309&VName=PQD

Siemaszko, C. (2012 May 3). Birmingham erupted into chaos in 1963 as battle for civil rights exploded in the South. Retrieved from http://www.nydailynews.com/news/national/birmingham-erupted-chaos-1963-battle-civil-rights-exploded-south-article-1.1071793

Simkim, J. (n.d.). Jim Crow laws. Spartacus Educational. Retrieved from http://www.spartacus.schoolnet.co.uk/USAjimcrow.htm

Social Security Online. (n.d.). Food stamps and other nutritional programs. Retrieved from http://www.ssa.gov/pubs/10100.html

Standlin, D. (2011, January 6). Velvet-voiced homeless man does intro for "today," reunites with mom. USATODAY Online, from http://www.usatoday.com/ communities/ondeadline/post/2011/01/homeless-man-with-golden-voice-does-the-intro-for-today-show-/1

Starling, K. (1998, March).The 10 biggest killers of blacks [Electronic version]. Ebony Magazine. Retrieved from http://findarticles.com/p/articles/ mi_m1077/is_n5_v53/

ai_20380710/

Steele, C. (1992, April). Race and the schooling of black Americans [Electronic version]. The Atlantic. Retrieved from http://www.theatlantic.com/past/docs/ unbound/flashbks/ blacked/steele.htm

Steuter, E., & Willis, D. (2008) At war with metaphor: Media, propaganda, and racism in the war on terror. Lanham, MD: Lexington Books.

Stevenson, B. (2014) Just mercy. https://www.goodreads.com/ book/show/20342617-just-mercy

Stevenson, B. (2015) Equal Justice Initiative. Bryan Stevenson talks to Oprah about why we need to abolish the death penalty. Retrieved from https://eji.org/news/bryan-stevenson-tells-oprah-winfrey-why-we-should-abolish-death-penalty/

Stillman, T. F., Baumeister, R. F., Lambert, N. M., Crescioni, A. W., DeWall, N., & Fincham, F. D. (2009, July). Alone and without purpose: Life loses meaning following social exclusion. National Institutes of Health. Retrieved from http://www.ncbi.nlm.nih.gov/pmc/articles/PMC2717555/

Stricker, F. (2007). How America lost the war on poverty-and how to win it. Chapel Hill, NC: University of North Carolina Press.

Sylvester, M. (1998). The African American: A Journey from Slavery to Freedom. Retrieved from Long Island University C. W. Post Campus http://www.liu.edu/cwis/CWP/library/aaslavry.htm

Taney, R. B. (n.d.). Dred Scott Case: The supreme court decision PBS.org. https://www.pbs.org/wgbh/aia/part4/4h2933.html

Taylor, E. (2010, September 9). Little-known black history fact:

The negro motorist green book. Retrieved from http:// www.blackamericaweb.com/ ?q=articles/news/the_black_ diaspora_news/21801

Thurow, L. (1969). Poverty and discrimination. Washington, DC: Brookings Institute Press.

Time Books: The culture of poverty. (1966, November 25). Time Magazine [Electronic version]. Retrieved from http://www. time.com/time/magazine/article/ 0,9171,843139,00.html

Transatlantic slave trade slavery and remembrance (n.d) United nations educational scientific and cultural organization http:// slaveryandremembrance.org/articles/article/?id=A0002

Troolin Amy https://study.com/academy/lesson/social-and-eco- nomic-life-in-early-modern-europe-peasantry-nobility-ear- ly-modern-economies.html

Turner C. H. (1974). From poverty to dignity. Garden City, NY: Anchor Press/Doubleday.

U.S. Census Bureau. About poverty highlights (Revised May 22, 2012). Retrieved from http://www.census.gov/hheswww/ poverty/about/overview/index.html

U.S. Census Bureau current population survey. (2009). POV35: Poverty thresholds by size of family and number of related children under 18 years: 2009. http://www .census.gov/ hhes/www/cpstables/032010/pov/new35_000.htm

U.S. Census Bureau. (2009).United States Poverty estimates from 2005-2009 [Data File]. Available from factfinder http:// factfinder.census.gov/servlet/ STTable? _bm=y&-geo_ id=01000US&-qr_name=ACS_2009_5YR_G00 _S1701&-

context =st&-ds_name=ACS_2009_5YR_G00_&-tree_
id=307&-redoLog=false&format=

UNICEF. Goals: Eradicate extreme poverty and hunger. (n.d.). Retrieved from http://www.unicef.org/mdg/poverty.html

Varshney, A. (2002). Poverty eradication and democracy in the developing world. Human development occasional papers series. Retrieved from http://hdr.undp.org/en/reports/global/hdr2002/papers/Varshney_2002.pdf

Ward, M. (2020). How decades of US welfare policies lifted up the white middle class and largely excluded Black Americans. https://www.businessinsider.com/welfare-policy-created-white-wealth-largely-leaving-black-americans-behind-2020-8

Wealth and Culture in the South US History. (n.d.). https://courses.lumenlearning.com/suny-ushistory1os2xmaster/chapter/wealth-and-culture-in-the-south/

Weiss, L. (2009, September). Unmarried women hit hard by poverty. Retrieved from http://www.americanprogress.org/issues/2009/09/census_women.html

What is the meaning of the name Kunta Kinte? (n.d.). Retrieved from http://www.blurtit.com/q556583.html

White House Presidents. (n.d.). Abraham Lincoln. Retrieved from http://www.whitehouse.gov/ about/presidents/abrahamlincoln

Williams, S. D. (2005). The church must make reparation for its role in slavery, segregation https://www.ncronline.org/news/opinion/church-must-make-reparation-its-role-slavery-segregation

Winters, M. A., & Greene, J. P. (2002, November) Public School
Graduation Rates in the United States. https://www.
manhattan-institute.org/html/public-school-gradua-
tion-rates-united-states-5809.html

Wise, C., & Wheat, D. (2009). https://ldhi.library.cofc.edu/exhibits/
show/african_laborers_for_a_new_emp/pope_nicolas_v_and_
the_portuguPope Nicolas V and the Portuguese slave trade.

YouTube-Roots: Breaking Kunta. Retrieved from http://www.you-
tube.com/ watch?v=H_A2o8ICcIQ

Made in the USA
Middletown, DE
24 May 2022

66147689R00109